Wealth Mastery

The Ultimate Guide to Financial Freedom

Tyler James Hughes

WEALTH MASTERY: THE ULTIMATE GUIDE TO FINANCIAL FREEDOM

BY

Tyler James Hughes

© Copyright 2023 by Printed Page Publishers - All rights reserved.

It is not legal to reproduce, duplicate, or transmit any part of this document in either electronic means or printed format. Recording of this publication is strictly prohibited.

Table Of Contents

Introduction

Module 1: Foundations of Financial Success

- Understanding Money Mindset
- Setting Financial Goals
- Creating a Personal Budget
- Managing Debt Effectively

Module 2: Building Wealth through Earned Income

- Maximizing Your Earning Potential
- Negotiating Salary and Benefits
- Freelancing and Side Hustles
- Entrepreneurship Essentials

Module 3: Investing for Long-Term Growth

- Introduction to Investing
- Stock Market Basics
- Real Estate Investment Strategies
- Diversification and Risk Management

Module 4: Passive Income Strategies

- Introduction to Passive Income
- Dividend Investing
- Rental Property Ownership
- Creating and Selling Digital Products

Module 5: Advanced Wealth-Building Techniques

- Tax Strategies for Wealth Accumulation
- Asset Protection and Estate Planning
- Leveraging Debt for Wealth Creation
- Building Generational Wealth

Module 6: Financial Freedom and Beyond

- Achieving Financial Independence
- Lifestyle Design and Freedom
- Giving Back and Impactful Philanthropy
- Continuing Your Wealth Journey

Introduction

Welcome to Wealth Mastery, your gateway to unlocking the secrets of financial success and achieving true abundance in your life. In this comprehensive course, we embark on a journey together to demystify the world of finance, empower you with essential knowledge, and equip you with practical strategies to build lasting wealth.

Are you tired of living paycheck to paycheck, burdened by debt, and feeling like you're stuck in a cycle of financial struggle? Or perhaps you're already on the path to financial stability but eager to accelerate your progress and reach new heights of prosperity? Wherever you are on your financial journey, Wealth Mastery is designed to meet you there and guide you toward your goals.

In this course, we believe that true wealth goes beyond mere monetary riches. It's about having the freedom to live life on your own terms, pursue your passions, and make a positive impact on the world around you. Whether your dreams involve traveling the world, starting a business, or supporting your loved ones, financial empowerment is the key that unlocks endless possibilities.

Our curriculum is carefully crafted to cover every aspect of wealth-building, from laying the foundations of financial literacy to mastering advanced strategies for wealth accumulation and preservation. Throughout the course, you'll dive deep into topics such as budgeting, investing, passive income generation, tax optimization, and more.

But Wealth Mastery is more than just a collection of lessons and lectures. It's a transformative experience that empowers you to take control of your financial future and design the life you've always dreamed of.

As you embark on this journey, we encourage you to approach it with an open mind, a willingness to learn, and a commitment to taking action. Remember, the road to wealth is not always easy, but with dedication, perseverance, and the right knowledge at your disposal, success is within reach.

So, are you ready to take the first step toward a future of abundance and prosperity? If so, then let's begin our journey together. Welcome to Wealth Mastery — where financial freedom awaits.

Module 1: Foundations of Financial Success

Welcome to Module 1 of Wealth Mastery: Foundations of Financial Success. In this module, we lay the groundwork for your journey towards financial freedom by focusing on essential principles and practices that form the bedrock of a solid financial foundation.

Lesson 1: Understanding Money Mindset
Explore the psychological factors that influence our relationship with money.
Identify limiting beliefs and mindset blocks that may be holding you back from financial success.
Learn strategies for cultivating a positive and abundance-oriented mindset.

Lesson 2: Setting Financial Goals
Understand the importance of setting clear, measurable financial goals.
Discover techniques for defining short-term and long-term financial objectives.
Learn how to create SMART (Specific, Measurable, Achievable, Relevant, Time-bound) goals that propel you towards your desired financial future.

Lesson 3: Creating a Personal Budget
Learn the fundamentals of budgeting and why it's essential for financial management.
Explore different budgeting methods and find the one that aligns with your lifestyle and goals.
Gain practical tips for tracking expenses, managing cash flow, and optimizing your budget for financial success.

Lesson 4: Managing Debt Effectively
Understand the different types of debt and their impact on your financial health.
Learn strategies for reducing and eliminating debt, including the debt snowball and debt avalanche methods.
Discover how to use debt strategically and responsibly to achieve your financial goals.

Throughout Module 1, you'll not only gain valuable knowledge but also practical tools and exercises to apply what you learn to your own financial situation. By mastering the foundational principles covered in this module, you'll be better equipped to navigate the complexities of personal finance and set yourself on the path to lasting financial success.

Get ready to transform your relationship with money and lay the groundwork for a future of abundance. Let's dive into: Module 1: Foundations of Financial Success.

Understanding Money Mindset

In our journey towards financial mastery, one of the most crucial aspects to explore and understand is our relationship with money. This intricate bond often shapes our financial decisions, attitudes, and ultimately, our level of success in managing wealth. Welcome to Lesson 1: Understanding Money Mindset, where we delve deep into the psychological underpinnings that influence our perception of money and how we can cultivate a mindset conducive to financial abundance.

The Power of Mindset

At its core, mindset refers to the collection of beliefs, attitudes, and assumptions that shape how we perceive the world and ourselves within it. When it comes to money, our mindset plays a significant role in determining our financial behavior and outcomes. Whether we hold beliefs of scarcity or abundance, fear or opportunity, these underlying attitudes can either propel us forward towards financial success or hold us back in a cycle of limitation.

Identifying Money Mindset Patterns

To begin understanding our money mindset, it's essential to take a reflective journey into our past experiences, upbringing, and cultural influences. Many of our beliefs about money are formed early in life through observations of our parents, societal messages, and personal experiences. These beliefs may manifest as subconscious patterns that influence our financial decisions without our awareness.

Common Money Mindset Patterns

Scarcity Mindset: The belief that there is never enough money to go around, leading to fear, hoarding, and a reluctance to take risks.

Abundance Mindset: The belief that there are ample opportunities for wealth creation, leading to confidence, generosity, and a willingness to invest in oneself and others.

Fear of Failure: The fear of making mistakes or losing money, which can paralyze decision-making and prevent taking necessary risks for growth.

Money Avoidance: The tendency to avoid thinking about or dealing with money-related issues, leading to procrastination and financial disorganization.

Money Worship: The belief that money is the key to happiness and self-worth, leading to materialism and a never-ending pursuit of wealth for validation.

Cultivating a Positive Money Mindset: The good news is that our money mindset is not fixed; it can be shifted and transformed with awareness and intentional effort. Here are some strategies to cultivate a positive money mindset:
Practice Gratitude: Focus on what you have rather than what you lack, and express gratitude for your financial blessings, no matter how small.

Challenge Limiting Beliefs: Identify and challenge any negative beliefs or self-imposed limitations around money, replacing them with empowering affirmations.

Visualize Success: Use visualization techniques to imagine yourself achieving your financial goals and embodying the mindset of abundance and success.

Surround Yourself with Positivity: Surround yourself with people who uplift and inspire you to grow financially, and consume content that reinforces positive money beliefs.

Continuous Learning: Invest in your financial education and seek out opportunities to expand your knowledge and skills in wealth-building strategies.

By embracing a positive money mindset, you'll not only transform your relationship with money but also unlock new possibilities for financial growth and fulfillment. Remember, true wealth begins from within, and by cultivating a mindset of abundance, you set the stage for a future of prosperity and abundance.

Challenging Limiting Beliefs

One of the most powerful tools in cultivating a positive money mindset is challenging and reframing limiting beliefs. These beliefs often lurk in the depths of our subconscious, subtly influencing our thoughts and actions around money. To challenge these beliefs, it's essential to bring them into the light of conscious awareness and examine their validity.

Start by identifying any recurring negative thoughts or beliefs you have about money. These could be statements like "I'll never be wealthy," "Money is evil," or "I'm not good with finances." Once you've identified these beliefs, ask yourself:

> Where did this belief come from?
> Is there evidence to support or refute this belief?
> How is this belief holding me back from achieving my financial goals?
> What would happen if I let go of this belief and adopted a more empowering one?
> By interrogating these beliefs with curiosity and openness, you can begin to dismantle

their hold on your mindset and replace them with more empowering alternatives. For example, "I'll never be wealthy" could be reframed as "I am capable of creating abundance in my life through smart financial decisions and hard work."

Practicing Visualization and Affirmations

Visualization and affirmations are powerful techniques for reprogramming your subconscious mind and reinforcing positive money beliefs. Visualization involves vividly imagining yourself achieving your financial goals and experiencing the emotions associated with success. Take time each day to visualize yourself living the life of abundance you desire, whether it's owning your dream home, traveling the world, or enjoying financial security.

Affirmations are positive statements that you repeat to yourself regularly to reinforce desired beliefs or behaviors. Craft affirmations that align with your financial goals and repeat them daily with conviction and belief. For example, "I am worthy of abundance and success," "Money flows to me effortlessly," or "I am a magnet for financial prosperity."

Surrounding Yourself with Positivity

The company we keep and the media we consume can have a significant impact on our mindset and beliefs about money. Surround yourself with people who inspire and uplift you to think bigger and pursue your financial goals. Seek out mentors, role models, and communities of like-minded individuals who share your vision for financial abundance.

Similarly, be mindful of the content you consume, whether it's books, podcasts, or social media. Choose content that reinforces positive money beliefs, offers practical financial advice, and inspires you to take action towards your goals. Limit exposure to negative or fear-based messages that can undermine your confidence and motivation.

Conclusion

Understanding and reshaping your money mindset is a foundational step towards achieving financial success and abundance. By challenging limiting beliefs, practicing visualization and affirmations, and surrounding yourself with positivity, you can cultivate a mindset that empowers you to create the wealth and prosperity you desire.

In the next lesson, we'll dive into the practical process of setting clear and achievable financial goals that align with your newfound mindset of abundance. Get ready to take the first steps towards turning your financial dreams into reality!

Setting Financial Goals

Welcome to Lesson 2 of Wealth Mastery: Setting Financial Goals. In this lesson, we will explore the importance of setting clear and achievable financial goals and provide you with the tools and strategies to define your objectives effectively.

Why Set Financial Goals?

Financial goals serve as the roadmap that guides your journey towards financial success. Without clear goals, it's easy to drift aimlessly and struggle to make meaningful progress towards your desired financial future. Setting goals provides focus, motivation, and a sense of purpose to your financial endeavors, helping you stay on track even when faced with challenges or setbacks.

The SMART Goal Framework

A well-defined financial goal is one that is SMART: Specific, Measurable, Achievable, Relevant, and Time-bound.

Specific: Clearly define what you want to achieve with your financial goal. Avoid vague or ambiguous objectives and be as specific as possible about what you want to accomplish.

Measurable: Your goal should include quantifiable criteria that allow you to track your progress and determine when you have successfully achieved it. Establish concrete metrics or milestones to measure your success along the way.

Achievable: Ensure that your goal is realistic and attainable given your current resources, skills, and circumstances. While it's essential to aim high, setting unrealistic goals can lead to frustration and discouragement.

Relevant: Your financial goal should align with your values, priorities, and long-term vision for your life. Consider whether the goal is meaningful and relevant to your overall financial well-being and personal aspirations.

Time-bound: Set a specific timeframe or deadline for achieving your goal. Having a clear deadline creates a sense of urgency and helps you stay focused and accountable to your objectives.

Types of Financial Goals

Financial goals can encompass a wide range of objectives, including:

Short-term Goals: Goals that you aim to accomplish within the next 1-3 years, such as building an emergency fund, paying off credit card debt, or saving for a vacation.

Medium-term Goals: Goals that you plan to achieve within the next 3-5 years, such as buying a home, starting a business, or funding your children's education.

Long-term Goals: Goals that require more extended time horizons, typically spanning 5 years or more, such as retiring comfortably, achieving financial independence, or leaving a legacy for future generations.

Exercise: Defining Your Financial Goals

Take some time to reflect on your financial aspirations and define your goals using the SMART framework. Consider the following questions:

What specific financial objectives do I want to achieve in the short-term, medium-term, and long-term?

How will I measure my progress towards each goal? What metrics or milestones will indicate success?

Are my goals realistic and attainable given my current financial situation, resources, and skills?

Do my goals align with my values, priorities, and long-term vision for my life?

What deadlines or timeframes will I set for each goal to create a sense of urgency and accountability?

By taking the time to define your financial goals thoughtfully, you set yourself up for success and lay the groundwork for a future of financial abundance and prosperity.

In the next lesson, we'll explore practical strategies for creating and implementing a personal budget that supports your financial goals and helps you achieve financial stability and freedom. Get ready to take control of your finances and turn your dreams into reality!

Developing Your Financial Blueprint

Now that you've defined your financial goals using the SMART framework, it's time to develop your personalized financial blueprint. Your financial blueprint serves as the roadmap that outlines the specific steps and strategies, you'll take to achieve each of your goals.

1. Break Down Your Goals into Actionable Steps:

For each of your financial goals, break them down into smaller, actionable steps or milestones. These smaller tasks make your goals more manageable and help you track your progress more effectively.
For example, if your goal is to save $10,000 for a down payment on a home within three years, break it down into yearly, monthly, or even weekly savings targets.

2. Prioritize Your Goals:

Not all goals are created equal, and it's essential to prioritize them based on their importance, urgency, and impact on your overall financial well-being.
Identify which goals are most critical to you and prioritize them accordingly. This ensures that you allocate your resources and efforts towards what matters most to you.

3. Create a Budget Aligned with Your Goals:

Your budget is a powerful tool that helps you allocate your income towards your financial goals and essential expenses while avoiding unnecessary spending.

Review your current spending habits and identify areas where you can cut back or optimize to free up more funds for your goals.

Allocate specific amounts of money towards each of your goals within your budget to ensure that you're making consistent progress towards them.

4. Implement Strategies to Increase Income:

In addition to managing expenses, consider implementing strategies to increase your income and accelerate your progress towards your financial goals.

This could involve negotiating a higher salary, pursuing career advancement opportunities, starting a side hustle or freelance business, or investing in income-generating assets.

5. Monitor Your Progress and Adjust as Needed:

Regularly monitor your progress towards your financial goals and adjust your strategies as needed based on changing circumstances or priorities.

Celebrate your achievements along the way, no matter how small, and use any setbacks or challenges as learning opportunities to course-correct and continue moving forward.

Conclusion: Taking Action Towards Financial Success

Setting financial goals is just the first step towards achieving financial success. It's the actions you take and the strategies you implement that ultimately determine whether you'll reach your goals. By developing a clear plan of action, prioritizing your goals, and consistently taking steps towards them, you'll be well on your way to turning your financial dreams into reality.

In the next lesson, we'll delve deeper into the practical aspects of creating and maintaining a personal budget that supports your financial goals and helps you achieve financial stability and freedom. Get ready to take control of your finances and embark on the path to wealth mastery!

Creating a Personal Budget

Welcome to Lesson 3 of Wealth Mastery, where we explore one of the most practical and essential tools for achieving financial success: the personal budget. A well-constructed budget is the foundation of financial management and a key element in turning your financial goals into reality. In this lesson, you will learn how to create and maintain a budget that aligns with your financial goals, keeps you on track, and provides clarity over your income, expenses, and savings.

Why Budgeting Is Crucial for Financial Success

Budgeting isn't about restricting your spending or limiting your enjoyment of life—it's about controlling your money so that it works for you. A personal budget gives you a clear picture of your financial health and allows you to allocate your resources in a way that reflects your goals and priorities. Without a budget, it's easy to fall into a pattern of overspending, accumulating debt, and feeling financially overwhelmed.

Benefits of Budgeting:

Increased Financial Awareness: A budget helps you see where your money is going, making you more conscious of your spending habits.

Achieving Financial Goals: By allocating money towards savings, investments, or debt repayment, a budget helps you make steady progress towards your short-term and long-term goals.

Control Over Spending: With a budget in place, you can identify areas where you might be overspending and redirect that money towards things that truly matter to you.

Reduced Stress: Knowing exactly how much money you have to cover your expenses reduces the anxiety and uncertainty that often accompanies financial management.

Building Financial Discipline: Regularly adhering to a budget builds discipline, a critical skill for long-term financial success.

Steps to Creating a Personal Budget

Step 1: Calculate Your Total Income

Before you can allocate your money, you need to know how much you're working with. Start by calculating your total monthly income, including:

Primary Income: Your take-home pay after taxes (net income).
Side Hustles or Freelancing: If you have additional streams of income, like a side hustle, freelance work, or any other form of part-time employment.
Passive Income: Money earned from investments, dividends, rental properties, or other passive income streams.

It's important to focus on net income—what you actually receive after taxes and deductions—because that's the money you have available to budget.

Step 2: Track and List All Expenses

To create a realistic budget, you must first know where your money is going. Categorize your expenses into two main categories:

Fixed Expenses:

These are predictable, regular expenses that stay the same each month, such as:

1. Rent or mortgage payments
2. Utilities (electricity, water, internet)
3. Insurance premiums (health, car, home)
4. Loan payments (car, student loans, personal loans)
5. Subscriptions or memberships

Variable Expenses:

These are costs that can fluctuate from month to month, such as:

6. Groceries
7. Dining out
8. Entertainment (movies, concerts, events)
9. Transportation (gas, public transit, ride-shares)
10. Clothing and personal care
11. Miscellaneous purchases

Tracking your spending for a month will give you a clear picture of your actual expenses. You can do this by reviewing bank statements, receipts, or using a budgeting app.

Step 3: Identify Discretionary and Non-Discretionary Spending

Once you have a detailed list of your expenses, separate them into two groups:

Non-Discretionary Expenses: These are essential expenses that you cannot eliminate or reduce significantly (e.g., rent, insurance, utility bills).

Discretionary Expenses: These are non-essential expenses that you can control or reduce (e.g., dining out, entertainment, travel).

This distinction is important because discretionary expenses are the areas where you can make adjustments if your budget is tight or if you want to allocate more money toward savings and financial goals.

Step 4: Set Spending Limits

Now that you know how much income you have and where your money is going, it's time to set spending limits in each category. This is where you allocate your income based on your priorities. A common method is the **50/30/20 rule**, which divides your budget as follows:

50% of Income for Needs: This includes essential expenses like housing, utilities, groceries, transportation, and healthcare.

30% of Income for Wants: This includes discretionary spending on entertainment, dining out, hobbies, vacations, and non-essential items.

20% of Income for Savings/Investments: This portion is dedicated to your financial goals, such as building an emergency fund, saving for retirement, or paying off debt.

You can adjust these percentages based on your personal financial situation and goals. For instance, if you're focused on paying off debt aggressively, you might allocate more than 20% toward that.

Step 5: Allocate Funds Toward Financial Goals

Now, align your budget with your financial goals. If you've set goals like saving for a down payment, paying off debt, or building an emergency fund, make sure a portion of your income is allocated to these areas each month.

For example:

Debt Repayment: If you have high-interest debt, prioritize it by allocating a larger portion of your income to paying it off quickly.
Emergency Fund: Aim to build an emergency fund that covers 3-6 months of living expenses. Allocate part of your monthly income towards this until you reach your target.
Investing and Retirement: If you're not already contributing to a retirement plan, start investing a percentage of your income in tax-advantaged accounts like a 401(k) or IRA.

Step 6: Review and Adjust Regularly

Creating a budget is not a one-time task. It requires regular review and adjustments to accommodate changes in your income, expenses, or financial goals. At the end of each month, review your budget and compare it to your actual spending. If you notice any discrepancies, analyze why they happened and make necessary adjustments for the following month.

Budgeting Methods

There are several budgeting methods you can adopt depending on your preferences and financial goals. Here are a few popular ones:

Zero-Based Budgeting: In this method, every dollar of your income is allocated to a specific category (needs, wants, savings, etc.), leaving you with a "zero" balance at the end of the month. This ensures that all your income is accounted for and used intentionally.

Envelope System: This is a cash-based system where you allocate physical cash into different envelopes for each spending category. Once the envelope is empty, you're done spending in that category for the month. It's a great method for those who want strict control over their spending.

50/30/20 Rule: As mentioned earlier, this simple rule helps divide your income into needs, wants, and savings, making it easy to manage.

Pay Yourself First: In this method, you prioritize savings by allocating a fixed percentage of your income to savings or investments first, before budgeting for other expenses. This method forces you to focus on financial goals rather than spending.

Tools to Help with Budgeting

There are numerous tools and apps available to help simplify the budgeting process. Some popular options include:

Mint: A free budgeting app that tracks all your bank accounts, credit cards, and bills in one place.

YNAB (You Need a Budget): A paid app that uses zero-based budgeting to help you allocate every dollar of your income.

EveryDollar: A budgeting tool based on Dave Ramsey's financial principles, focusing on tracking spending and budgeting with intention.

Conclusion: Empowering Yourself with a Personal Budget

Creating and sticking to a personal budget is one of the most effective ways to take control of your finances, avoid debt, and achieve your financial goals. Remember, a budget is a living document—it's flexible and adaptable as your financial situation changes. By building a budget that aligns with your goals and values, you're taking an essential step towards mastering your financial future.

In the next lesson, we'll explore strategies for managing and reducing debt, one of the biggest obstacles to financial freedom. With a solid budget in place, you'll be well-equipped to tackle your debt and move closer to financial independence!

Managing and Reducing Debt

Welcome to Lesson 4 of Wealth Mastery, where we focus on one of the most significant barriers to financial freedom: debt. Debt, if unmanaged, can be a heavy burden that limits your ability to save, invest, and achieve financial independence. In this lesson, you'll learn strategies for managing and reducing debt, so you can free yourself from its constraints and move towards a more secure financial future.

The Impact of Debt on Your Financial Health

Debt in itself is not inherently bad; it's how you manage it that determines its effect on your financial health. Some forms of debt, like a mortgage or business loan, can be considered "good debt" if they help you acquire assets or investments that appreciate over time. However, high-interest consumer debt, such as credit card balances or payday loans, can quickly spiral out of control, making it difficult to achieve financial goals.

Common Types of Debt:

Credit Card Debt: High-interest debt that accumulates if you carry a balance month to month. Credit card debt is one of the most expensive forms of debt.

Student Loans: Education loans that can take decades to repay if not managed properly.

Mortgage: A long-term loan to finance the purchase of a home. While necessary for many, a large mortgage can strain your finances if not properly managed.

Auto Loans: Loans used to finance vehicles, which depreciate in value over time.

Personal Loans: Often used for consolidating debt or covering large expenses, these loans come with varying interest rates depending on creditworthiness.

How Debt Affects Your Financial Future

Excessive debt reduces your ability to save, invest, or achieve other financial goals. The more debt you carry, the more of your income is allocated towards servicing it (paying off interest and principal). This limits your disposable income and can create stress or restrict your lifestyle.

Additionally, large amounts of debt can negatively impact your credit score, making it more expensive to borrow money in the future or even impacting your ability to secure housing, employment, or lower insurance rates.

Debt Management Strategies

Effectively managing and reducing debt requires both a disciplined approach and the right strategies. Let's explore some practical steps you can take to regain control of your finances.

Step 1: Understand the Totality of Your Debt

The first step in managing debt is gaining a clear understanding of how much you owe and to whom. Make a list of all your debts, including:

- The total balance of each loan or credit card
- The interest rate associated with each debt
- The minimum monthly payment required
- Any upcoming deadlines or terms

Having a comprehensive overview of your debt allows you to prioritize which debts to tackle first.

Step 2: Prioritize High-Interest Debt

Once you have a list of all your debts, prioritize them based on their interest rates. Focus on paying off high-interest debt first, such as credit card balances or payday loans. These types of debt often accumulate the most interest, making it harder to pay them off over time.

Debt Avalanche vs. Debt Snowball

There are two popular debt repayment methods to consider:

Debt Avalanche: Focuses on paying off debts with the highest interest rate first while making minimum payments on other debts. This method saves you the most money on interest over time.

Example: If you have a credit card with 18% interest and a student loan with 5% interest, you'd prioritize paying off the credit card first.

Debt Snowball: Focuses on paying off the smallest balances first, regardless of interest rates. Once the smallest debt is paid off, you roll the amount you were paying on that debt into the next smallest debt. This method helps build momentum and motivation.

Example: If you have a $500 credit card debt and a $5,000 student loan, you'd tackle the smaller $500 debt first, even if the interest rate is lower.

Choose the method that best suits your financial situation and personality. The Debt Avalanche saves more money on interest, but the Debt Snowball can provide psychological wins by clearing smaller debts quickly.

Step 3: Consolidate Debt (If Applicable)

If you have multiple high-interest debts, consider consolidating them into a single loan with a lower interest rate. This simplifies your payments and can lower the overall interest you pay.

Debt Consolidation Loans: A personal loan used to pay off multiple debts, leaving you with one loan to manage.

Balance Transfer Credit Cards: These cards allow you to transfer high-interest credit card debt to a new card with a low or 0% introductory interest rate. However, be sure to pay off the balance before the introductory period ends, or you could be hit with high rates again.

Home Equity Loans: If you own a home, you might be able to take out a home equity loan at a lower interest rate to pay off high-interest debt. This option can be risky, as it puts your home on the line if you can't make the payments.

Step 4: Create a Debt Repayment Plan

A solid repayment plan is key to eliminating debt systematically. Here's how to create one:

Determine Your Budget for Debt Repayment: Based on your personal budget (from Lesson 3), determine how much of your monthly income can be allocated towards paying down debt. Aim to pay more than the minimum payment whenever possible.

Automate Payments: Set up automatic payments for your debts to ensure you never miss a payment, which can result in fees and damage to your credit score.

Cut Unnecessary Spending: Redirect money from non-essential expenses towards your debt repayment plan. This might involve cutting back on dining out, entertainment, or luxury items temporarily until your debts are paid off.

Increase Income: If possible, increase your income by taking on a side hustle, freelance work, or selling unused items. This extra cash can be applied to your debt, speeding up your repayment process.

Step 5: Renegotiate or Refinance Debt

In some cases, you may be able to negotiate better terms for your debt or refinance it at a lower interest rate.

Contact Creditors: If you're struggling with payments, reach out to your creditors to negotiate lower interest rates or more manageable repayment terms. Many creditors prefer to work with you rather than risk a default.

Refinancing Loans: If you have student loans, auto loans, or a mortgage, consider refinancing to secure a lower interest rate. Refinancing can reduce your monthly payments and save you money over the life of the loan.

Step 6: Avoid Accumulating New Debt

As you work to pay off your current debts, it's essential to avoid accumulating new debt. This might involve limiting credit card use, resisting impulse purchases, and sticking to your budget. If you must use credit cards, ensure that you can pay off the balance in full each month to avoid interest charges.

Understanding and Improving Your Credit Score

Your credit score plays a significant role in your financial life, influencing everything from loan approvals to interest rates. Understanding how your debt affects your credit score can help you improve it over time.

Payment History: Timely payments have the most significant impact on your credit score. Ensure that you never miss a payment, as this can severely damage your score.

Credit Utilization: Keep your credit card balances low compared to your credit limit. A credit utilization rate under 30% is generally recommended for maintaining a good credit score.

Length of Credit History: The longer your credit history, the better. Avoid closing old accounts, even if you no longer use them, as this can shorten your credit history.

Credit Inquiries: Be cautious about applying for new credit frequently, as multiple hard inquiries on your credit report can lower your score.

Conclusion: Taking Control of Your Debt

Managing and reducing debt requires commitment and discipline, but the rewards are immense. By gaining control over your debt, you free up more of your income to invest, save, and achieve your financial goals. Debt doesn't have to be a permanent burden—you can take charge and work towards financial independence.

Module 2: Building Wealth through Earned Income

Overview:

This module focuses on strategies to maximize and diversify your active income. While saving and investing are critical, increasing your earned income is a powerful way to accelerate your wealth-building journey. We'll cover topics like negotiating salary and benefits, freelancing and side hustles, and essential steps for starting your own business. The goal is to help you generate more income while keeping your financial and career goals in focus.

Lesson 1: Maximizing Your Earning Potential

In this first lesson, we explore the importance of maximizing your primary source of income—your career or job. This lesson will help you understand how to evaluate your worth in the marketplace, continuously develop your skills, and position yourself for promotions or raises.

Key Topics:

Self-Assessment of Skills and Market Value:

How to evaluate your skills and expertise relative to your industry.
Using platforms like LinkedIn, Glassdoor, or PayScale to compare your salary and job title to the industry standard.
Identifying areas where you can improve to increase your market value.

Continuous Learning and Professional Development:

Why lifelong learning is crucial for career growth and higher earning potential.
Free and paid resources to enhance skills (e.g., online courses, certifications, mentorship).
Leveraging professional networks for career advancement and new opportunities.

Strategic Career Moves:

Understanding when to switch jobs or industries for better opportunities.
Evaluating company benefits, culture, and long-term growth potential when considering career moves.

Building a Strong Personal Brand:

How to develop a personal brand that highlights your strengths and differentiates you in the job market.
Using social media, blogs, and industry events to showcase your expertise.

Lesson 2: Negotiating Salary and Benefits

Negotiating your salary and benefits is a key factor in building wealth through earned income. Many people leave money on the table because they don't negotiate. In this lesson, you'll learn how to confidently negotiate a better salary, bonuses, and benefits package.

Key Topics:

Preparing for Negotiation:

Researching salary data to know your worth.

Timing your negotiation (e.g., performance reviews, after securing a job offer).
Understanding non-monetary benefits that can be negotiated (e.g., vacation days, remote work flexibility, professional development opportunities).

Salary Negotiation Tactics:

How to frame your value to the employer.
Overcoming objections and how to use positive leverage in salary discussions.
Handling counteroffers and deciding whether to accept, reject, or ask for more.

Negotiating Benefits and Perks:

Beyond salary: negotiating for bonuses, stock options, and retirement contributions.
Health and wellness benefits: health insurance, gym memberships, mental health support.
Time-related perks: paid vacation, sick leave, and flexible working hours.

Post-Negotiation Strategy:

Assessing the negotiation outcome and next steps.
What to do if your employer doesn't budge, and when to consider looking for new opportunities.
Creating a long-term negotiation strategy for future raises.

Lesson 3: Freelancing and Side Hustles

Freelancing and side hustles are great ways to increase your earned income outside of your full-time job. This lesson dives into how you can identify lucrative freelance opportunities or side hustles, balance them with your primary job, and scale them into sustainable income streams.

Key Topics:

Identifying Freelance and Side Hustle Opportunities:

How to identify marketable skills you can monetize (e.g., graphic design, writing, coding, consulting).
Popular freelance platforms and how to get started (e.g., Upwork, Fiverr, Freelancer).
Evaluating demand in your niche and targeting high-paying clients.

Setting Up Your Side Hustle:

Building a side hustle without disrupting your main job.
Time management strategies for balancing multiple income streams.
Setting goals and milestones for your side hustle, whether it's earning extra cash or growing it into a full-time business.

Pricing Your Freelance Services:

How to price your services based on skill level, demand, and value to the client.
Negotiating freelance rates and understanding different pricing models (e.g., hourly vs. project-based).

Scaling a Side Hustle:

Strategies for scaling your side hustle or freelance work, including outsourcing tasks or increasing your rates.
Managing client relationships and building a portfolio or client base.
Transitioning from side hustle to full-time business, if desired.

Lesson 4: Entrepreneurship Essentials

Entrepreneurship can be one of the fastest ways to build significant wealth, but it requires careful planning and execution. This lesson will cover the basics of starting and growing a business, including how to turn an idea into a profitable venture.

Key Topics:

Finding and Validating a Business Idea:

Identifying profitable business ideas by solving problems or meeting needs in the market.
How to validate your idea before investing time and money (e.g., surveys, MVPs, pre-sales).
Understanding your target audience and creating a business model that serves them.

Setting Up Your Business:

Legal aspects of starting a business: registering a company, setting up business accounts, and obtaining licenses.
Building a strong brand and online presence through websites, social media, and digital marketing.
Managing cash flow, creating a business plan, and setting financial goals.

Growing and Scaling Your Business:

Strategies for acquiring your first customers and building a loyal customer base.
Scaling operations: expanding your product or service line, hiring employees, and automating key processes.
Diversifying revenue streams and exploring new market opportunities.

Entrepreneurial Mindset and Risk Management:

Developing the mindset for entrepreneurial success: persistence, resilience, and adaptability.

Understanding business risks and how to manage them (e.g., cash flow, competition, market downturns).
Long-term growth: strategic planning and goal-setting for business expansion.

Conclusion: Building Wealth through Earned Income

By the end of Module 2, you'll have the tools to increase your active income through career advancement, negotiation, freelancing, and entrepreneurship. Maximizing your earned income is a critical step in accelerating your wealth-building journey. With the strategies learned in this module, you'll be better positioned to increase your financial stability, grow your savings, and fund future investments.

This module is essential for anyone looking to take control of their income and create multiple streams of revenue, paving the way for financial independence.

Maximizing Your Earning Potential

Maximizing your earning potential is a critical component of wealth-building. Whether you're working in a traditional job, freelancing, or starting a business, increasing your income is the fastest way to accelerate your financial growth. In this lesson, we'll explore practical steps you can take to ensure that you're earning what you're worth and continuously growing your income over time.

1. Assessing Your Market Value

Understanding your worth in the job market is the first step toward maximizing your income. Often, people settle for less than they could be earning simply because they haven't taken the time to evaluate their skills, experience, and how they compare to others in their industry.

How to Assess Your Market Value:

   Research Salary Data: Use tools like PayScale, Glassdoor, or LinkedIn Salary Insights to see what others in similar roles are earning. This can give you a benchmark for where your salary should be.
   Industry Standards: Be aware of the industry norms, as salary ranges can vary widely between different fields. For example, software engineers, healthcare professionals, and financial analysts may have different earning potential based on demand, location, and expertise.
   Geographic Considerations: Salaries vary significantly by location. For example, tech roles in San Francisco may pay much higher than the same roles in smaller cities. Understanding these differences can help you make strategic decisions about where to live or work remotely.

How to Increase Your Market Value:

Skill Development: Continually improving your skills is a surefire way to increase your value. Take advantage of online courses, certifications, and workshops that are relevant to your industry.

Networking: Building relationships in your industry can open up new opportunities for career advancement or higher-paying jobs. Attend conferences, join online communities, and actively engage on platforms like LinkedIn.

Showcasing Your Achievements: Employers value measurable results. Keep a record of your achievements (e.g., successful projects, revenue you've generated, cost-saving initiatives) and use them to strengthen your case when negotiating for a raise or promotion.

2. Lifelong Learning and Professional Development

In a rapidly changing job market, staying stagnant is not an option if you want to maximize your income potential. Continuous learning is key to keeping your skills relevant and in demand. Employers and clients value professionals who demonstrate a commitment to self-improvement and innovation.

Ways to Enhance Your Skills:

Take Online Courses: Platforms like Coursera, Udemy, and LinkedIn Learning offer affordable courses in a wide range of subjects, from leadership and communication to technical skills like programming or digital marketing.

Earn Certifications: For certain industries, certifications can greatly increase your market value. For example, certifications in project management (e.g., PMP), digital marketing (e.g., Google Analytics), or financial analysis (e.g., CFA) are highly valued.

Stay Updated with Industry Trends: Subscribe to industry publications, listen to podcasts, and follow thought leaders to stay on top of the latest trends. This knowledge will not only help you remain relevant but also position you as an expert in your field.

Building Specialized Skills:

Focus on developing a skill set that's in high demand but underrepresented in your current workplace or industry. Specialization, whether in a niche field of technology, data science, or creative industries, can command significantly higher wages.

Leadership Skills:

Learning how to manage people and projects effectively can set you apart from your peers. Leadership positions often come with higher salaries and additional benefits.

3. Strategic Career Moves

Maximizing your earning potential often requires making strategic moves in your career. This could involve switching companies, moving to a new city, or even changing industries. People who stay in the same job for too long may limit their earning potential, as salary increases are often more significant when you change employers.

Switching Jobs for Higher Pay:

    Leverage Job Offers: If you've received a job offer elsewhere, you can use it as leverage to negotiate a higher salary in your current position. Even if you don't intend to leave, the offer provides proof of your value in the marketplace.

    Timing Your Move: There are strategic moments to seek promotions or job changes, such as after completing a major project or during annual reviews. Timing your career moves can significantly impact your earning trajectory.

    Industry Shift: If you feel capped in your current industry, explore sectors that may have more growth potential. For example, transitioning from traditional finance to fintech or from a general IT role to cybersecurity could provide higher earnings and long-term job security.

    Evaluating Company Culture and Benefits: Beyond salary, a company's culture and benefits package play a key role in maximizing your long-term financial health. Look for companies that offer comprehensive retirement plans (e.g., 401(k) matching), health benefits, bonuses, stock options, and opportunities for career growth.

4. Building a Personal Brand

In today's competitive job market, having a strong personal brand can set you apart and make you more attractive to potential employers, clients, or business partners. A personal brand is how you present yourself, your values, and your expertise to the world.

How to Build a Strong Personal Brand:

    Create a Professional Online Presence: Ensure that your LinkedIn profile is up to date and reflects your skills, achievements, and career goals. Share relevant articles, engage in discussions, and connect with industry leaders.

    Content Creation: Establish yourself as a thought leader by creating content in your field. This could be in the form of blog posts, articles, podcasts, or social media content. Sharing valuable insights can help you build authority in your industry.

    Portfolio and Testimonials: Showcase your work through a portfolio or website, especially if you're in a creative or freelance industry. Client testimonials and case studies add credibility and demonstrate the value you provide.

    Networking and Mentorship: Building relationships with mentors and peers in your industry can open doors to new opportunities, collaborations, and higher-paying roles. A strong network is often key to learning about job openings or freelance opportunities that aren't advertised publicly.

    Attend Industry Events: Conferences, seminars, and workshops are excellent opportunities to meet influential people, stay updated on industry trends, and strengthen your professional reputation.

5. Overcoming Career Plateaus

At some point, many professionals experience a career plateau where promotions or raises seem harder to attain. To overcome these plateaus, you need to take proactive steps toward growth.

Breaking Through a Plateau:

Ask for Feedback: Seek constructive feedback from supervisors or peers to identify areas where you can improve and grow.

Seek New Challenges: Take on new responsibilities or projects that are outside your comfort zone. This will not only help you develop new skills but also demonstrate leadership and initiative.

Consider Further Education: If you find that your current education level is holding you back from higher-paying roles, consider going back to school for an advanced degree or relevant certification.

Conclusion: Maximizing Your Earning Potential

Maximizing your earning potential is not just about working harder—it's about working smarter. By assessing your market value, continuously developing your skills, making strategic career moves, building a strong personal brand, and breaking through career plateaus, you can significantly increase your income over time.

As you move forward, remember that earning more allows you to save and invest more, accelerating your journey toward financial freedom. Take ownership of your career, focus on growth, and you'll be well on your way to achieving wealth mastery.

Negotiating Salary and Benefits

Negotiating your salary and benefits is one of the most powerful yet underutilized tools in building long-term wealth. Many professionals leave money on the table by not negotiating, either because they don't know how or they're uncomfortable doing so. In this lesson, you'll learn how to effectively negotiate your salary, benefits, and perks, positioning yourself for maximum financial growth in your career.

1. Why Salary Negotiation is Crucial

Your salary forms the foundation of your wealth-building strategy. The more you earn, the more you can save, invest, and grow your financial assets over time. While many people focus on budgeting and cutting costs, increasing your income—especially through salary negotiations—can have a far greater impact on your financial future.

Key Statistics on Salary Negotiation:

According to research, individuals who negotiate their salary earn more than those who don't—often by as much as **$5,000 to $10,000** annually.

Over the course of a career, negotiating a higher salary just once can lead to hundreds of thousands of dollars in additional earnings.

Even small salary increases compound over time as they affect your future raises, retirement contributions, bonuses, and job offers. With the right approach, you can increase your lifetime earning potential significantly by mastering salary negotiations.

2. Preparing for Salary Negotiation

Preparation is key to a successful salary negotiation. You need to enter the conversation with a clear understanding of your value, the industry standard, and the best timing for negotiation.

Assessing Your Market Value:

Research Comparable Salaries: Use platforms like **Glassdoor**, **PayScale**, **LinkedIn Salary Insights**, or even industry reports to benchmark salaries for your role, experience level, and location. This helps ensure you're asking for a reasonable amount based on market trends.

Factor in Location: Salaries vary by region, with urban areas typically offering higher pay due to the cost of living. Remote work opportunities can also provide leverage, as some companies are willing to offer higher pay to attract top talent from other regions.

Understand Your Unique Value: What do you bring to the table that sets you apart from others? This could be specific skills, certifications, experience, or measurable results from past roles (e.g., increased sales, cost savings, process improvements).

Timing the Negotiation:

    Best Times to Negotiate: Negotiating after receiving a job offer is ideal, but existing employees can also negotiate during performance reviews, after completing a major project, or when taking on new responsibilities.

    Don't Wait Too Long: If you wait until after you've accepted a job offer, it becomes much harder to negotiate. You want to engage in this discussion before officially signing any contracts.

3. How to Conduct a Salary Negotiation

Once you've done your research and identified your market value, it's time to prepare for the actual negotiation. Approach this conversation with confidence and clarity, as employers expect salary discussions and often leave room in the budget for negotiation.

Step-by-Step Guide to Salary Negotiation:

Express Enthusiasm for the Job:

Start the conversation on a positive note by expressing your excitement about the role and your desire to contribute to the company's success. This demonstrates that you're not just looking for more money, but you're genuinely interested in the opportunity.

State Your Research:

Clearly explain that you've done your homework by researching the market value for your position. Mention the range of salaries for similar roles based on the information you've gathered and why you believe your desired salary is fair based on your experience and the job's responsibilities.

Give a Salary Range:

It's often best to provide a salary range rather than a fixed number, with your ideal salary being near the bottom of that range. For example, if you want to earn $80,000, you might say you're looking for something in the range of $80,000 to $90,000. This allows room for negotiation while still anchoring the conversation in your favor.

Justify Your Request:

Be prepared to explain why you're asking for a specific salary. Highlight your past achievements, skills, and unique qualifications. Provide examples of how you've positively impacted previous employers (e.g., increased revenue, improved efficiency, etc.).

Pause and Listen:

After stating your case, be comfortable with silence. Give the employer time to process your request and respond. It's essential not to rush this part of the conversation, as employers may come back with a higher offer if given time to reflect.

Handling Objections:

If the employer says they can't meet your salary request, don't immediately accept the offer. Ask follow-up questions like, "Can we revisit this conversation in six months?" or "Are there other forms of compensation we can explore?"
Be ready to negotiate other benefits if salary isn't flexible (more on that below).

4. Negotiating Benefits and Perks

Salary isn't the only component of compensation. In many cases, benefits and perks can be just as valuable, or even more so, depending on your needs. When salary negotiations stall, shifting the focus to benefits can still allow you to gain valuable concessions.

Key Benefits to Negotiate:

Bonuses:

Annual bonuses, signing bonuses, or performance-based bonuses are great alternatives to a higher base salary. These can sometimes be easier for companies to offer because they are not fixed recurring costs.

Stock Options or Equity:

For startups or rapidly growing companies, stock options or equity can be a lucrative part of the compensation package. Ask if there are opportunities to invest in the company or receive equity as part of your compensation.

Retirement Contributions:

Ensure that your employer is contributing to a retirement fund, such as a 401(k) or pension plan. You can also ask if the company offers matching contributions, which can greatly accelerate your retirement savings.

Health and Wellness Benefits:

Health insurance is a major expense for most people. Ask about health plans, dental and vision coverage, and health savings accounts (HSAs). Wellness benefits like gym memberships, mental health support, or wellness stipends can also add value.

Paid Time Off (PTO):

Negotiating for more vacation days, paid sick leave, or the ability to work remotely can add considerable value. Work-life balance is increasingly important to employees, and many companies are open to being flexible in this area.

Professional Development:

Ask for the company to sponsor your continued education or professional development through courses, certifications, or conferences. Investing in your growth can increase your future earning potential.

5. After the Negotiation: Next Steps

Once you've completed the negotiation, it's important to ensure that everything is properly documented. Ask for the final offer in writing, including salary, bonuses, benefits, and any other negotiated terms. Review it carefully before accepting.

What to Do If Negotiation Fails:

Not all negotiations will end with a higher offer, but don't be discouraged. If your employer cannot meet your salary request, ask for a timeline for future raises and review opportunities. You can also use the negotiation as leverage when seeking opportunities elsewhere. Having the experience of negotiating makes you better equipped for future discussions.

6. Developing a Long-Term Negotiation Strategy

Negotiating your salary and benefits is not a one-time event—it's an ongoing process that continues throughout your career. The key is to approach it strategically.

Long-Term Salary Growth Tips:

    Regular Performance Reviews: Schedule regular reviews with your manager to discuss your progress and contributions. These reviews are great opportunities to ask for raises and promotions.

    Proactive Career Development: Always be working on improving your skills and taking on new challenges that demonstrate your value. This keeps you in a strong position to negotiate when the time comes.

    Keep an Eye on the Market: Regularly check salary benchmarks for your role, especially if you've been in the same position for several years. This ensures that you're keeping pace with industry standards.

Conclusion: Mastering Salary and Benefits Negotiation

Salary negotiation is one of the most powerful tools you have for increasing your income and accelerating your wealth-building journey. By preparing thoroughly, conducting confident negotiations, and leveraging benefits, you can unlock significant financial opportunities that go far beyond your initial job offer.

The strategies you've learned in this lesson will help you not only negotiate a better salary today but set you up for ongoing success in future roles and industries. Remember, wealth is built not just by earning more but by making smart decisions with the income you have—starting with negotiating what you deserve.

Freelancing and Side Hustles

In today's economy, relying solely on a traditional job for income is no longer the only path to financial stability or wealth. Freelancing and side hustles have become increasingly popular ways for individuals to diversify their income streams, gain financial independence, and pursue their passions. In this lesson, we'll explore how to effectively start and manage a freelancing career or side hustle, ensuring it becomes a valuable component of your wealth-building strategy.

1. Understanding the Freelance Economy

The freelance economy has grown exponentially in recent years. With advances in technology and the rise of remote work, more people are choosing to become freelancers or take on side gigs. According to a report by **Upwork**, about **36%** of the U.S. workforce is freelancing, and this number is expected to grow.

Benefits of Freelancing and Side Hustles:

Flexibility: You can choose when and where you work, allowing you to balance personal commitments and other responsibilities.

Control Over Income: As a freelancer, you have the opportunity to set your rates and take on as many projects as you can handle, potentially leading to a higher income than a traditional job.

Skill Diversification: Freelancing allows you to develop new skills and broaden your experience in various industries, making you more marketable in the long run.

2. Identifying Your Skills and Niche

Before diving into freelancing or starting a side hustle, it's crucial to identify your unique skills and find a niche that aligns with your strengths and interests. This step will not only increase your chances of success but also ensure that you enjoy the work you're doing.

Steps to Identify Your Skills:

Self-Assessment: Take time to reflect on your current skills, hobbies, and interests. What are you passionate about? What skills do you possess that others may need?

Market Research: Look at freelance job platforms such as **Upwork**, **Fiverr**, and **Freelancer** to see what skills are in high demand. Identify the types of projects that excite you and have a steady demand.

Networking: Talk to friends, family, or professional contacts about your skills. They may offer insights into what they believe you excel at and what potential clients might need.

Finding Your Niche:

Specialization: While it's tempting to offer a broad range of services, specializing in a particular area can help you stand out. Consider what unique value you can provide based on your skills and market demand.

Combine Skills: Sometimes, combining two or more skills can create a unique niche. For example, if you're skilled in graphic design and have experience in digital marketing, you could specialize in creating marketing materials for small businesses.

3. Setting Up Your Freelancing Business

Once you've identified your skills and niche, it's time to set up your freelancing business. This involves creating a strong brand, establishing an online presence, and developing a portfolio to showcase your work.

Creating Your Brand:

Choose a Business Name: Select a professional name that reflects your services and is easy to remember.

Design a Logo: A well-designed logo can help establish your brand identity. Use online tools like **Canva** or hire a designer from freelance platforms to create a logo that resonates with your target audience.

Establishing an Online Presence:

Build a Website: Having a personal website acts as your digital portfolio. Include information about your services, a portfolio of your work, testimonials from clients, and a blog to showcase your expertise.

Utilize Social Media: Leverage social media platforms to promote your services and connect with potential clients. Platforms like LinkedIn, Instagram, and Twitter can help you build a following and attract clients in your niche.

Building a Portfolio:

Showcase Your Work: Include samples of your work that demonstrate your skills and expertise. If you're just starting and don't have client work to showcase, consider creating mock projects that reflect your style and capabilities.

Collect Testimonials: Reach out to past clients, colleagues, or even friends who can vouch for your skills. Positive testimonials can significantly boost your credibility.

4. Finding Clients and Projects

Finding clients is often the most challenging aspect of freelancing, especially for beginners. However, there are several strategies you can employ to attract clients and secure projects.

Freelance Job Platforms:

    Utilize Online Marketplaces: Websites like **Upwork**, **Fiverr**, and **Freelancer** are great places to find freelance gigs. Create a compelling profile and apply for projects that align with your skills.

    Create Service Listings: On platforms like Fiverr, you can create service listings (known as "gigs") where clients can directly purchase your services.

Networking:

    Leverage Your Network: Inform your friends, family, and professional contacts that you're offering freelance services. Personal recommendations can lead to new clients.

    Attend Networking Events: Participate in industry conferences, meetups, and workshops to meet potential clients and fellow freelancers. Networking can open doors to new opportunities and collaborations.

Cold Outreach:

    Identify Potential Clients: Research businesses or individuals who could benefit from your services. Create a list of prospects to target.

    Craft Personalized Pitches: Send personalized emails or messages outlining how your services can solve a specific problem for them. Highlight your unique value proposition and include links to your portfolio.

5. Setting Your Rates

One of the most critical aspects of freelancing is determining how much to charge for your services. Setting your rates too low can lead to burnout and undervalue your work, while charging too high can scare potential clients away.

Factors to Consider When Setting Rates:

    Market Research: Investigate what others in your niche are charging. This will give you a benchmark for setting competitive rates.

    Your Experience and Skills: If you have specialized skills or extensive experience, you can justify higher rates. Conversely, beginners may need to start lower to attract initial clients.

    Cost of Living: Consider your location and the cost of living when setting rates. Ensure your rates align with your financial needs and goals.

Pricing Models:

Hourly Rate: Charging by the hour is common in many freelance industries. Be clear about how you track your hours and communicate your rate upfront.

Project-Based Pricing: For certain projects, a flat fee can be more appealing to clients. This model can also give you the potential to earn more if you complete projects efficiently.

Retainers: Some freelancers establish retainer agreements with clients for ongoing work. This provides a stable income stream while allowing clients to budget for your services.

6. Managing Your Freelance Business

Once you start securing clients and projects, managing your freelance business effectively is crucial to its long-term success. This includes maintaining organization, managing finances, and ensuring high-quality work.

Organization and Time Management:

Use Project Management Tools: Tools like **Trello**, **Asana**, or **Todoist** can help you manage tasks, deadlines, and project details. Staying organized will ensure you meet client expectations and deadlines.

Set Boundaries: Freelancing often leads to a blurred line between personal and professional time. Set specific working hours and stick to them to maintain a healthy work-life balance.

Financial Management:

Track Income and Expenses: Keep meticulous records of all income and expenses related to your freelance business. This is vital for tax purposes and overall financial health.

Set Aside Money for Taxes: As a freelancer, you're responsible for paying your taxes. Set aside a percentage of your income regularly to avoid a financial shock during tax season.

Invest in Your Business: Consider reinvesting a portion of your earnings into tools, courses, or marketing strategies that will help you grow your freelance business.

7. Scaling Your Freelance Business

As your freelancing career progresses, you may want to consider ways to scale your business for increased income and opportunities. This could involve expanding your services, collaborating with others, or developing passive income streams.

Expanding Your Services:

Upselling: Offer additional services to existing clients based on their needs. For example, if you design websites, you might also offer ongoing website maintenance or SEO services.

Diversification: Consider branching out into related fields that complement your current services. For instance, if you're a graphic designer, you could expand into video editing or social media management.

Collaborating with Other Freelancers:

Team Up: Partnering with other freelancers can help you take on larger projects or offer a broader range of services. Collaborations can lead to more significant opportunities and shared resources.

Passive Income Opportunities:

Create Digital Products: Consider developing and selling digital products, such as e-books, online courses, or templates related to your area of expertise. These can generate passive income and help establish you as an authority in your niche.
Affiliate Marketing: Promote products or services relevant to your audience and earn commissions through affiliate marketing. This can be done via a blog, social media, or email marketing.

Conclusion: Embracing Freelancing and Side Hustles

Freelancing and side hustles can significantly enhance your earning potential, diversify your income sources, and accelerate your journey to wealth mastery. By identifying your skills, establishing a strong brand, and effectively managing your freelance business, you can create a fulfilling and profitable career outside of traditional employment.

As you embark on your freelancing journey, remember that success takes time and persistence. Stay adaptable, keep learning, and embrace the opportunities that come your way. With dedication and a strategic approach, freelancing can become a valuable asset in your wealth-building strategy.

Entrepreneurship Essentials

Entrepreneurship is one of the most effective ways to build wealth and achieve financial independence. Starting your own business allows you to create a product or service that aligns with your passions, capitalize on market opportunities, and ultimately control your financial destiny. In this lesson, we will explore the essentials of entrepreneurship, from identifying business ideas to launching and growing your venture.

1. Understanding Entrepreneurship

Entrepreneurship is the process of designing, launching, and running a new business, often with the goal of making a profit. Entrepreneurs take on the risks associated with starting and managing a business, but they also reap the rewards when their ventures succeed.

Key Traits of Successful Entrepreneurs:

Visionary Thinking: Successful entrepreneurs can envision a product, service, or solution that fills a gap in the market. They think outside the box and are willing to take calculated risks.

Resilience: Entrepreneurship involves overcoming challenges and setbacks. Resilience is crucial to navigating the ups and downs of building a business.

Adaptability: The ability to pivot and adapt to changing market conditions is essential. Successful entrepreneurs stay attuned to market trends and are willing to modify their business strategies accordingly.

Passion and Commitment: A strong passion for their work fuels entrepreneurs through difficult times. Commitment to their vision keeps them focused and motivated.

2. Identifying Business Ideas

The first step in your entrepreneurial journey is identifying a viable business idea. This requires a combination of self-reflection, market research, and creativity.

Sources for Business Ideas:

Personal Passion and Skills: Start by reflecting on what you love to do and what skills you possess. Successful businesses often arise from entrepreneurs who are passionate about their work.

Market Gaps: Conduct market research to identify gaps in existing products or services. Look for areas where customer needs are not being met.

Trends and Innovations: Stay informed about industry trends, emerging technologies, and innovations. Trends can provide inspiration for new business ideas or improvements to existing offerings.

Brainstorming Techniques:

Mind Mapping: Use mind maps to visualize your thoughts and ideas. Start with a central theme and branch out to related ideas and concepts.

SWOT Analysis: Conduct a SWOT (Strengths, Weaknesses, Opportunities, Threats) analysis to evaluate potential business ideas. This framework helps identify the viability of an idea based on internal and external factors.

3. Creating a Business Plan

A well-structured business plan is essential for guiding your entrepreneurial journey and securing funding if needed. It serves as a roadmap for your business, outlining your goals, strategies, and financial projections.

Components of a Business Plan:

Executive Summary: Provide a concise overview of your business idea, including your mission statement and the problem your business solves.
Market Analysis: Conduct thorough research on your target market, competitors, and industry trends. Define your target audience and explain how you plan to reach them.
Marketing and Sales Strategy: Outline your marketing and sales strategies, including how you will promote your business, attract customers, and generate sales.
Financial Projections: Include detailed financial projections, such as startup costs, revenue forecasts, and profit margins. This section is crucial for attracting investors and lenders.
Operational Plan: Describe the day-to-day operations of your business, including staffing, production processes, and supply chain management.

Business Plan Resources:

Business Plan Templates: Utilize templates from platforms like **SBA.gov** or **Score.org** to help structure your plan.
Business Plan Software: Consider using business plan software like **LivePlan** or **Bizplan** to create a professional-looking plan.

4. Securing Funding for Your Business

Funding is often a critical aspect of launching a new venture. Depending on the nature of your business, you may need to secure capital to cover startup costs.

Funding Options:

Self-Funding: Many entrepreneurs start by funding their business with personal savings or income from their current job. This option allows you to maintain full control of your business.
Friends and Family: You can seek financial support from friends and family who believe in your vision. Be transparent about the risks and expectations involved.
Loans: Traditional bank loans or microloans can provide the necessary capital to start your business. Prepare your business plan to present to potential lenders.
Investors: Attracting investors can provide significant capital in exchange for equity in your business. Prepare a compelling pitch to showcase your business opportunity.
Crowdfunding: Online platforms like **Kickstarter** and **Indiegogo** allow you to raise funds from a large number of people in exchange for early access to your product or service.

5. Launching Your Business

Once you have a solid business plan and funding in place, it's time to launch your business. This stage involves executing your plan and beginning operations.

Steps to Launch Your Business:

    Register Your Business: Choose a business structure (e.g., sole proprietorship, LLC, corporation) and register your business with the appropriate government authorities.

    Create Your Brand Identity: Develop a brand identity that reflects your values and resonates with your target audience. This includes designing a logo, creating a website, and establishing your social media presence.

    Develop Your Product or Service: Finalize the development of your product or service, ensuring it meets quality standards and customer expectations.

    Set Up Operations: Establish your operational processes, including supply chain management, production, and customer service.

Marketing Your Business:

    Build an Online Presence: Utilize social media, email marketing, and content marketing to build brand awareness and attract customers.

    Leverage Influencer Marketing: Collaborate with influencers in your industry to promote your product or service to a broader audience.

    Network and Attend Events: Attend industry conferences, trade shows, and networking events to connect with potential clients and partners.

6. Growing Your Business

Once your business is up and running, the next step is to focus on growth. This involves expanding your customer base, increasing sales, and enhancing your product or service offerings.

Strategies for Growth:

    Diversification: Consider diversifying your product or service offerings to appeal to a broader audience. This can involve creating new products or entering new markets.

    Customer Retention: Focus on building strong relationships with existing customers. Implement loyalty programs, offer exceptional customer service, and seek feedback to improve your offerings.

    Scaling Operations: As demand grows, evaluate ways to scale your operations efficiently. This may involve automating processes, hiring additional staff, or investing in technology.

7. Overcoming Challenges in Entrepreneurship

Entrepreneurship is not without its challenges. Being prepared to navigate obstacles is crucial for long-term success.

Common Challenges:

- **Financial Management**: Managing cash flow and budgeting can be difficult for new entrepreneurs. Regularly review your finances and consider hiring a professional accountant if needed.
- **Competition**: Competition can be fierce in many industries. Stay informed about your competitors and continuously improve your offerings to maintain a competitive edge.
- **Work-Life Balance**: The demands of entrepreneurship can lead to burnout if not managed properly. Set boundaries and prioritize self-care to maintain a healthy work-life balance.

Conclusion: The Path to Entrepreneurial Success

Entrepreneurship offers a powerful avenue for building wealth and achieving financial independence. By identifying viable business ideas, creating a solid business plan, securing funding, and implementing effective marketing strategies, you can turn your entrepreneurial vision into reality.

As you embark on your entrepreneurial journey, remember that success requires persistence, adaptability, and a willingness to learn from your experiences. Embrace the challenges and celebrate the victories, knowing that each step brings you closer to mastering wealth and financial freedom.

Module 3: Investing for Long-Term Growth

Investing is a powerful tool for building wealth over time. This module will cover the fundamentals of investing, including an introduction to various investment vehicles, the basics of the stock market, real estate investment strategies, and the importance of diversification and risk management. By the end of this module, you will have a solid understanding of how to invest for long-term growth and how to make informed financial decisions.

Lesson Breakdown

Lesson 1: Introduction to Investing

Understanding the importance of investing for wealth building.
Different types of investments (stocks, bonds, real estate, mutual funds).
Setting investment goals and developing a personal investment strategy.

Lesson 2: Stock Market Basics

Overview of how the stock market works.
Understanding stocks, bonds, and mutual funds.
Key concepts such as market capitalization, dividends, and price-to-earnings ratio.

Lesson 3: Real Estate Investment Strategies

Different types of real estate investments (residential, commercial, REITs).
Strategies for successful real estate investing (buy-and-hold, flipping, rental properties).
Analyzing the pros and cons of real estate as an investment.

Lesson 4: Diversification and Risk Management

The importance of diversification in an investment portfolio.
Understanding risk tolerance and how to assess it.
Strategies for managing risk and protecting your investments.

Lesson 1: Introduction to Investing

In this lesson, we will explore the fundamental principles of investing and why it is essential for achieving long-term financial growth.

1. The Importance of Investing for Wealth Building

Investing is the act of allocating resources, usually money, in order to generate income or profit. Unlike saving, which involves putting money aside for future use, investing involves using that money to create additional wealth.

Why Invest?

Compound Growth: Investing allows your money to grow over time through the power of compounding. This means that not only does your initial investment grow, but the returns you earn also generate additional returns.

Inflation Hedge: Inflation erodes the purchasing power of your money over time. Investing can help you stay ahead of inflation and maintain your purchasing power.

Achieving Financial Goals: Whether saving for retirement, buying a home, or funding education, investing provides a path to achieve long-term financial objectives.

2. Types of Investments

Investing can take many forms, and it's essential to understand the various types of investment vehicles available.

Common Types of Investments:

Stocks: Shares of ownership in a company. Investors can profit through capital appreciation (increase in stock price) and dividends (periodic payments to shareholders).

Bonds: Debt securities issued by governments or corporations. Investors earn interest over time and receive the principal back at maturity.

Mutual Funds: Investment vehicles that pool money from multiple investors to invest in a diversified portfolio of stocks, bonds, or other securities. Managed by professional fund managers.

Real Estate: Investing in physical properties to generate rental income or capital appreciation.
Exchange-Traded Funds (ETFs): Similar to mutual funds but traded on stock exchanges. ETFs typically track a specific index or sector.

3. Setting Investment Goals

Before investing, it's essential to define your financial goals and develop a strategy that aligns with them.

Steps to Set Investment Goals:

Define Your Objectives: Determine what you are investing for (e.g., retirement, purchasing a home, funding education).

Time Horizon: Consider how long you plan to invest. Different goals may require different investment strategies.

Risk Tolerance: Assess how much risk you are willing to take. Understanding your comfort level with market fluctuations is critical in shaping your investment strategy.

4. Developing a Personal Investment Strategy

A well-defined investment strategy helps you stay focused on your goals and navigate market fluctuations.

Components of an Investment Strategy:

Asset Allocation: Decide how to distribute your investments across different asset classes (stocks, bonds, real estate) based on your risk tolerance and time horizon.

Investment Style: Choose between active investing (frequent buying and selling) and passive investing (long-term buy-and-hold strategy).

Monitoring and Adjusting: Regularly review your investment performance and make adjustments as needed to stay aligned with your goals.

5. Different Investment Strategies

Understanding various investment strategies can help you decide how to allocate your assets effectively. Each strategy has its own set of risks and rewards.

Common Investment Strategies:

Value Investing: This strategy involves identifying undervalued stocks that are trading for less than their intrinsic value. Investors seek to buy these stocks and hold them until the market recognizes their true value. Prominent value investors include Warren Buffett and Benjamin Graham.

Growth Investing: Growth investors focus on companies that are expected to grow at an above-average rate compared to their industry or the overall market. These companies may reinvest profits into expansion, and growth investors often look for stocks with high price-to-earnings ratios and strong revenue growth.

Income Investing: This strategy emphasizes generating a steady stream of income from investments, typically through dividends or interest payments. Income investors often choose dividend-paying stocks, bonds, or real estate investment trusts (REITs) to create a reliable income source.

Index Investing: This passive investment strategy involves investing in index funds or ETFs that track a specific market index, such as the S&P 500. Index investing aims to replicate the performance of the index rather than trying to outperform it.

Dollar-Cost Averaging: This strategy involves consistently investing a fixed amount of money into a particular investment over time, regardless of its price. Dollar-cost averaging can help reduce the impact of market volatility by spreading out the investment over different price points.

6. The Impact of Market Cycles

Understanding market cycles is essential for making informed investment decisions. Markets experience cycles of expansion and contraction, influenced by various economic factors.

Phases of Market Cycles:

Expansion: During this phase, the economy is growing, businesses are investing, and consumer confidence is high. Stock prices tend to rise, and investments in equities often yield strong returns.

Peak: The peak occurs when the economy reaches its maximum output, and market sentiment is overly optimistic. This phase may be characterized by inflated asset prices and excessive risk-taking.

Contraction (Recession): In this phase, economic activity slows, leading to decreased corporate profits and rising unemployment. Investors may experience declining stock prices and reduced investment returns.

Trough: The trough is the lowest point of the economic cycle, where sentiment is typically pessimistic. This phase can present opportunities for investors to buy undervalued assets as prices may be significantly lower.

7. Importance of Continuous Learning and Education

Investing is a constantly evolving field, and staying informed is crucial for success. Continuous learning allows investors to adapt to changing market conditions, emerging trends, and new investment opportunities.

Ways to Enhance Your Investment Knowledge:

Books and Online Courses: Read books by renowned investors, financial experts, and economists. Online platforms like Coursera, Udemy, and Khan Academy offer courses on investing and finance.

Podcasts and Webinars: Listen to investment-related podcasts or attend webinars hosted by industry professionals to gain insights and tips from experts.

Financial News and Research: Stay updated with financial news from reputable sources like Bloomberg, CNBC, and The Wall Street Journal. Access research reports and analysis from financial institutions to inform your investment decisions.

Networking: Join investment clubs or online forums to connect with other investors. Sharing experiences and discussing strategies can provide valuable perspectives.

8. Getting Started with Investing

As you begin your investing journey, it's important to take actionable steps to put your knowledge into practice.

Steps to Start Investing:

Assess Your Financial Situation: Before you invest, evaluate your financial health, including your savings, debt, and expenses. Ensure you have an emergency fund in place.

Open an Investment Account: Choose a brokerage firm or investment platform that suits your needs. Research options based on fees, account types, and available investment products.

Start Small: If you're new to investing, consider starting with a small amount of money. Many platforms allow you to invest with minimal initial capital. This approach allows you to learn and grow your investment skills over time.

Stay Disciplined: Stick to your investment strategy and avoid making impulsive decisions based on market fluctuations. Patience and discipline are key traits of successful investors.

Lesson 2: Stock Market Basics

In this lesson, we will delve into the fundamentals of the stock market, exploring how it operates the different types of stocks, key terminology, and the mechanics of buying and selling stocks. Understanding these concepts is crucial for making informed investment decisions and navigating the stock market effectively.

What is the Stock Market?

The stock market is a collection of markets and exchanges where the buying and selling of publicly traded company shares occurs. It serves as a platform for investors to purchase ownership in companies and is a critical component of the global economy.

Functions of the Stock Market:

Capital Raising: Companies can raise capital by issuing shares to the public through initial public offerings (IPOs). This capital can be used for expansion, research and development, and other business needs.

Liquidity: The stock market provides liquidity to investors, allowing them to easily buy and sell shares. This liquidity helps investors quickly convert their investments into cash when needed.

Price Discovery: The stock market facilitates the process of price discovery, where the prices of stocks are determined based on supply and demand dynamics. Factors such as company performance, market conditions, and investor sentiment influence stock prices.

How the Stock Market Works

The stock market operates through a network of exchanges, where buyers and sellers come together to trade stocks. The two primary types of stock exchanges are:

Primary Market: This is where new shares are created and sold for the first time through IPOs. Companies offer shares to the public to raise capital, and investors can purchase these shares directly from the issuer.

Secondary Market: Once shares have been issued in the primary market, they are traded among investors in the secondary market. This includes exchanges like the New York Stock Exchange (NYSE) and NASDAQ, where investors buy and sell existing shares.

Market Participants:

    Investors: Individuals or institutions that buy shares with the expectation of earning a return on their investment.

    Brokers: Intermediaries who facilitate the buying and selling of stocks on behalf of investors. Brokers can be traditional firms or online platforms.

    Market Makers: Firms that ensure liquidity in the market by being ready to buy and sell stocks at publicly quoted prices. They help facilitate smooth trading.

Types of Stocks

    Stocks can be classified into various categories based on different criteria. Here are some common types:

Common Stocks vs. Preferred Stocks:

Common Stocks: Represent ownership in a company and entitle shareholders to vote on corporate matters. Common stockholders may receive dividends, but these payments are not guaranteed.

Preferred Stocks: Hold a higher claim on assets and earnings than common stocks. Preferred shareholders receive fixed dividends before common shareholders and have a higher priority in the event of liquidation.

Growth Stocks vs. Value Stocks:

Growth Stocks: Shares of companies expected to grow at an above-average rate compared to their industry. These companies typically reinvest earnings into the business rather than paying dividends.

Value Stocks: Shares of companies that are considered undervalued relative to their intrinsic value. Value investors seek stocks that are trading for less than their true worth, with the expectation that the market will eventually recognize their value.

Large-Cap, Mid-Cap, and Small-Cap Stocks:

Large-Cap Stocks: Companies with a market capitalization of $10 billion or more. These stocks are typically well-established and less volatile.

Mid-Cap Stocks: Companies with a market capitalization between $2 billion and $10 billion. These stocks offer a balance of growth potential and stability.

Small-Cap Stocks: Companies with a market capitalization under $2 billion. Small-cap stocks can offer higher growth potential but are generally more volatile.

Key Stock Market Terminology

Familiarizing yourself with stock market terminology is essential for effective communication and understanding of the market. Here are some key terms:

Market Capitalization: The total market value of a company's outstanding shares. It is calculated by multiplying the stock price by the number of shares outstanding.

Dividends: Payments made by a company to its shareholders, usually from profits. Dividends can be distributed in cash or additional shares.

Earnings Per Share (EPS): A measure of a company's profitability calculated by dividing net income by the number of outstanding shares. EPS is a key indicator for evaluating a company's financial health.

Price-to-Earnings Ratio (P/E Ratio): A valuation ratio calculated by dividing a company's current share price by its earnings per share. The P/E ratio helps investors assess whether a stock is overvalued or undervalued.

Bull Market: A market condition characterized by rising stock prices and investor optimism. It often reflects a strong economy and increased investor confidence.

Bear Market: A market condition characterized by falling stock prices and pessimism among investors. It often occurs during economic downturns or periods of uncertainty.

How to Buy and Sell Stocks

Buying and selling stocks can be done through brokerage accounts, which allow investors to execute trades in the stock market. Here are the basic steps to buying and selling stocks:

Opening a Brokerage Account:

Choose a Broker: Research and select a brokerage firm that fits your needs. Consider factors like fees, account types, available investment products, and customer service.

Complete the Application: Fill out the necessary forms to open an account, which may require personal information, financial details, and identification.

Fund Your Account: Transfer money into your brokerage account to start trading. This can typically be done via bank transfer, wire transfer, or check.

Placing a Trade:

Research Stocks: Conduct research to identify stocks you want to buy or sell. Utilize tools such as stock screeners, analyst reports, and financial news.

Choose Order Type: When placing a trade, decide on the type of order you want to use:

Market Order: Buy or sell a stock at the current market price. This type of order is executed immediately.

Limit Order: Specify the price at which you are willing to buy or sell a stock. The order will only be executed if the stock reaches that price.

Monitor Your Investment: After executing a trade, monitor the performance of your investment. Consider setting stop-loss orders to protect your investment from significant losses.

The Psychology of Investing

Understanding the psychology of investing is crucial for making sound investment decisions. Emotional factors often play a significant role in how investors behave in the stock market.

Common Psychological Traps:

Fear of Missing Out (FOMO): The anxiety that one might miss a profitable investment opportunity can lead to impulsive decisions. Investors may rush to buy into a stock that has recently surged in price without proper analysis.

Loss Aversion: Research shows that people tend to fear losses more than they value gains. This can lead to holding onto losing stocks for too long in the hope of a rebound or selling winning stocks too early to lock in profits.

Herd Mentality: Many investors tend to follow the crowd, buying stocks that are popular or in the news without conducting their own research. This behavior can drive prices up unsustainably and lead to significant losses when the market corrects.

Overconfidence: Some investors overestimate their knowledge and ability to predict market movements. This can result in taking on excessive risk and making poor investment choices.

Strategies for Managing Emotions:

Develop a Plan: Create a comprehensive investment plan that outlines your goals, risk tolerance, and investment strategy. Having a clear plan can help you stay focused and reduce emotional decision-making.

Stick to Your Strategy: Avoid making impulsive trades based on market fluctuations or news headlines. Trust in your research and strategy, and remain disciplined.

Limit Exposure to Market Noise: While it's essential to stay informed, constant exposure to financial news can heighten anxiety. Consider limiting the time spent consuming market news and focus on your long-term goals instead.

The Importance of Market Research and Analysis

Successful investing relies heavily on thorough research and analysis. Understanding market trends, company performance, and broader economic factors can help you make informed investment decisions.

Types of Analysis:

Fundamental Analysis: This approach involves evaluating a company's financial health by analyzing financial statements, earnings reports, and other key indicators. Fundamental analysts look for companies with strong fundamentals that may be undervalued by the market.

Technical Analysis: Technical analysis focuses on historical price movements and trading volumes to predict future price behavior. Chart patterns, indicators, and trends are utilized to identify potential buying or selling opportunities.

Sentiment Analysis: This method assesses investor sentiment and market psychology. Analysts may gauge market sentiment through surveys, social media, and news articles to understand how it may influence stock prices.

Conducting Research:

Use Financial Ratios: Ratios such as the P/E ratio, debt-to-equity ratio, and return on equity provide valuable insights into a company's financial performance and risk profile.

Read Earnings Reports: Quarterly and annual earnings reports provide essential information about a company's performance, revenue growth, and future outlook. Pay attention to guidance from management regarding future earnings expectations.

Follow Industry Trends: Staying informed about industry trends and competitive dynamics can help you assess potential risks and opportunities for your investments.

Practical Tips for New Investors

Starting your investment journey can be overwhelming, but with the right approach, you can navigate the stock market more effectively. Here are some practical tips to help new investors succeed:

Start with a Budget: Determine how much money you can afford to invest without impacting your financial stability. It's wise to start small and gradually increase your investment as you gain confidence and knowledge.

Educate Yourself: Continuously educate yourself about investing principles, strategies, and market trends. Utilize books, online courses, podcasts, and other resources to enhance your understanding.

Diversify Your Portfolio: Avoid putting all your money into a single stock or sector. Diversification can help mitigate risk and improve overall portfolio performance.

Consider Dollar-Cost Averaging: Instead of trying to time the market, consider investing a fixed amount regularly (e.g., monthly) regardless of market conditions. This approach can help smooth out market volatility and reduce the impact of short-term price fluctuations.

Review and Rebalance: Periodically review your investment portfolio to ensure it aligns with your goals and risk tolerance. If certain investments have grown significantly or underperformed, consider rebalancing your portfolio to maintain your desired asset allocation.

Be Patient: Investing is a long-term endeavor. Avoid chasing short-term gains and focus on your long-term financial goals. Remember that markets can be volatile, and patience is often rewarded.

Conclusion

In this lesson, we covered the fundamental concepts of the stock market, including its functions, types of stocks, key terminology, and the mechanics of buying and selling stocks. We also explored the psychological aspects of investing, the importance of research and analysis, and practical tips for new investors.

Understanding these principles will help you navigate the stock market with confidence and make informed investment decisions. In the next lesson, we will dive into real estate investment strategies, exploring how to leverage real estate as a source of wealth creation. Remember, successful investing requires a commitment to continuous learning and discipline in your approach.

In the next lesson, we will explore real estate investment strategies, diving into various approaches to building wealth through real estate. As you continue your investment journey, remember that informed decision-making is key to successful investing. Stay curious, keep learning, and remain disciplined in your approach.

Lesson 3: Real Estate Investment Strategies

Real estate investment is one of the most proven methods for building long-term wealth. This lesson will explore the different strategies available for real estate investing, how to assess property value, financing options, and the risks and rewards associated with this asset class.

Why Invest in Real Estate?

Real estate has been a cornerstone of wealth creation for centuries due to its potential for income generation, appreciation, and tax advantages. Real estate can provide stability, act as a hedge against inflation, and offer diversification to your investment portfolio.

Benefits of Real Estate Investing:

Cash Flow: Real estate investments can generate regular income through rental payments, which can help cover expenses and provide additional cash flow.

Appreciation: Over time, properties often appreciate in value, allowing investors to sell them for a profit. This appreciation can be due to factors like market conditions, improvements in the local area, or upgrades to the property.

Leverage: Real estate allows for the use of leverage, meaning you can purchase a property using borrowed funds (e.g., a mortgage), which can amplify your returns.

Tax Advantages: Real estate investors can take advantage of various tax deductions, including mortgage interest, depreciation, property taxes, and maintenance costs, reducing their overall tax burden.

Common Real Estate Investment Strategies

There are several ways to invest in real estate, each with its own risk profile and potential for returns. Here are some of the most common strategies:

Buy and Hold:

Overview: The buy-and-hold strategy involves purchasing a property and holding it for an extended period, typically renting it out to generate income while benefiting from long-term appreciation.

Pros: Steady rental income, long-term appreciation, potential tax benefits.

Cons: Requires property management, illiquidity, and market volatility may affect property values.

Fix and Flip:

Overview: Fix-and-flip investors purchase properties at a discount, make improvements, and sell them for a profit. This strategy focuses on short-term gains from property appreciation after renovation.

Pros: High potential returns in a short period, flexible exit strategy.

Cons: High risk due to market fluctuations, renovation costs can exceed expectations, requires expertise in property improvements.

Real Estate Investment Trusts (REITs):

Overview: REITs are companies that own, operate, or finance income-generating real estate across various sectors (e.g., residential, commercial, industrial). Investors can buy shares of REITs, providing exposure to real estate without directly owning property.

Pros: Liquidity (since REITs trade on stock exchanges), diversification, and regular dividend income.

Cons: Lower control over assets, performance is influenced by broader stock market trends.

Vacation Rentals (Short-Term Rentals):

Overview: This strategy involves renting out properties on platforms like Airbnb or VRBO. Investors capitalize on short-term rental demand in popular tourist areas, generating high rental income.

Pros: High potential income, flexibility to use the property personally, tax deductions.

Cons: Requires frequent management, susceptible to local regulations, seasonal demand can affect cash flow.

House Hacking:

Overview: House hacking involves living in one part of a property while renting out the other parts (e.g., a duplex or multifamily home). This allows the owner to reduce their living expenses or even live for free.

Pros: Reduced living costs, cash flow generation, entry into real estate investing with lower risk.

Cons: Being a landlord while living on the property, tenant issues, and property maintenance responsibilities.

Commercial Real Estate:

Overview: Investing in commercial properties (e.g., office buildings, retail spaces, industrial warehouses) provides the opportunity for higher returns compared to residential real estate. Commercial leases are often long-term, offering stability.

Pros: Higher potential returns, long-term leases, less hands-on management.

Cons: Higher entry costs, more complex regulations, vulnerable to economic cycles.

Assessing Property Value

Properly assessing a property's value is essential for making a sound real estate investment. Understanding the factors that influence property value can help you avoid overpaying and maximize returns.

Key Factors Influencing Property Value:

Location: The location of a property is one of the most significant factors affecting its value. Properties in desirable areas with access to amenities like schools, public transportation, and shopping centers tend to appreciate more over time.

Comparable Sales (Comps): Real estate agents and appraisers use recent sales of similar properties (comps) to estimate a property's value. Look for comps that match your target property in terms of size, condition, and location.

Market Trends: The overall real estate market can influence property values. In a seller's market, prices tend to rise due to higher demand, while in a buyer's market, property prices may stagnate or decline.

Property Condition: A well-maintained property with modern amenities and upgrades is likely to be valued higher than a property in poor condition. Renovations and improvements can increase property value and attract higher rental income.

Income Potential: For rental properties, the amount of rental income a property can generate is a critical factor in determining its value. Investors use metrics like the gross rental yield and capitalization rate (cap rate) to assess profitability.

Financing Options for Real Estate

Real estate often requires a significant upfront investment, but various financing options are available to help investors purchase properties.

Common Financing Options:

Traditional Mortgages: The most common way to finance real estate is through a mortgage from a bank or credit union. Mortgage terms vary, but they typically require a down payment (usually 20%) and have fixed or adjustable interest rates.

Hard Money Loans: These short-term loans are typically used by fix-and-flip investors. Hard money loans have higher interest rates and shorter terms than traditional mortgages but are often easier to qualify for.

FHA Loans: Federal Housing Administration (FHA) loans are available to first-time homebuyers and require a lower down payment (as low as 3.5%). These loans are a good option for house hackers who plan to live in part of the property.

Private Money Lenders: Private individuals or companies can offer financing for real estate deals. Terms and interest rates vary widely, but private money lenders are often more flexible than traditional banks.

Seller Financing: In some cases, the property seller may act as the lender, allowing the buyer to make payments directly to them over time. This option is often used when traditional financing is difficult to obtain.

Risks and Rewards of Real Estate Investing

While real estate can be a lucrative investment, it comes with its own set of risks. Understanding these risks can help you make more informed decisions.

Risks:

Market Fluctuations: Real estate values can decline due to economic downturns, oversupply in the market, or changes in demand. Investors must be prepared for short-term volatility.

Vacancies: Rental properties may experience periods of vacancy, reducing cash flow and potentially leading to financial strain if the property is leveraged.

Maintenance and Repairs: Property maintenance and unexpected repairs can erode profits. Investors must account for ongoing maintenance costs when evaluating potential returns.

Legal and Regulatory Issues: Zoning laws, property taxes, and local regulations can impact the profitability of real estate investments. Additionally, tenant laws can affect how you manage rental properties.

Rewards:

Wealth Accumulation: Over time, real estate tends to appreciate in value, contributing to significant wealth accumulation for long-term investors.

Passive Income: Rental properties provide a source of passive income, which can continue even as the property appreciates.

Tax Advantages: Real estate offers numerous tax benefits, including deductions for mortgage interest, depreciation, and operating expenses, which can reduce taxable income.

Conclusion

Real estate investment offers a range of strategies and opportunities for building long-term wealth. From buy-and-hold properties to fix-and-flip projects and even passive investments in REITs, there is a strategy to suit almost any investor's goals and risk tolerance.

In this lesson, we've covered the most common real estate investment strategies, how to assess property value, financing options, and the risks and rewards of investing in real estate. The next lesson will focus on Diversification and Risk Management, where we'll explore how to structure your investment portfolio to minimize risk while maximizing returns.

Lesson 4: Diversification and Risk Management

In this final lesson of Module 3, we'll focus on one of the most critical aspects of investing: diversification and risk management. Successful investors know that while the potential for high returns is alluring, managing risk is essential to sustaining long-term growth. This lesson will cover the principles of diversification, strategies to manage risk, and how to build a balanced investment portfolio.

Understanding Diversification

Diversification is the process of spreading your investments across various asset classes and financial instruments to reduce exposure to any single asset's risk. The idea is that different assets will perform differently in various market conditions, so having a mix of investments can smooth out overall portfolio performance.

Why Diversification is Important:

Reduces Risk: If all your investments are in one asset class, such as stocks, your portfolio is more vulnerable to downturns in that market. Diversification helps protect against significant losses by balancing the risks across various types of assets.

Increases Stability: A well-diversified portfolio tends to be more stable over time. When one asset class underperforms, another may perform well, helping to offset potential losses.

Maximizes Returns: While reducing risk, diversification doesn't mean you sacrifice returns. A balanced portfolio that includes a mix of high-growth and stable assets can achieve long-term growth with lower volatility.

Types of Diversification:

Asset Class Diversification: This involves investing in different asset classes such as stocks, bonds, real estate, and commodities. Each asset class has its own risk and return characteristics, and they often perform differently in various market environments.

Geographic Diversification: Geographic diversification involves investing in different regions or countries. Economic conditions vary across the globe, and diversifying internationally can reduce risk related to country-specific issues such as economic recessions or political instability.

Sector Diversification: Within an asset class like stocks, it's crucial to diversify across various sectors (e.g., technology, healthcare, finance). This ensures that if one sector experiences a downturn, the impact on your overall portfolio is minimized.

Company Size Diversification: Investing in companies of various sizes (small-cap, mid-cap, and large-cap) adds another layer of protection. Smaller companies may offer higher growth potential, while larger companies tend to be more stable.

Building a Diversified Portfolio

Constructing a diversified portfolio requires an understanding of your financial goals, risk tolerance, and time horizon. A balanced portfolio will typically include a mix of stocks, bonds, real estate, and other asset classes based on these factors.

Steps to Building a Diversified Portfolio:

Determine Your Risk Tolerance: Your risk tolerance depends on factors like your age, financial situation, and comfort level with market fluctuations. Younger investors with a longer time horizon may choose a more aggressive portfolio, while those nearing retirement may prefer a conservative approach.

Choose a Mix of Asset Classes: Based on your risk tolerance, allocate your investments across different asset classes. A typical diversified portfolio might include:

- **Stocks:** For long-term growth potential.
- **Bonds:** For stability and income generation.
- **Real Estate:** For both income (rental properties) and capital appreciation.
- **Commodities:** Such as gold or oil, for protection against inflation.

Consider Index Funds or ETFs: Index funds and exchange-traded funds (ETFs) are excellent options for diversifying within an asset class. These funds pool money from many investors to buy a broad range of assets, offering diversification without the need to purchase individual stocks or bonds.

Monitor and Rebalance: Over time, the value of different assets in your portfolio will change, causing your original allocation to shift. Periodically review your portfolio and rebalance it by buying or selling assets to maintain your desired allocation.

Example of a Diversified Portfolio:

For an investor with moderate risk tolerance and a long-term investment horizon, a diversified portfolio might look like this:

- 50% in stocks (including domestic and international stocks, large-cap and small-cap)
- 30% in bonds (both government and corporate bonds)
- 10% in real estate (either directly owned properties or REITs)
- 10% in commodities (such as gold or other tangible assets)

Risk Management Strategies

Managing risk is essential to protect your wealth, especially during volatile market conditions. In addition to diversification, there are several strategies investors can use to manage risk effectively.

1. Asset Allocation:

Asset allocation refers to how you distribute your investments across different asset classes. It's one of the most important factors in determining your portfolio's risk and return profile. A more aggressive asset allocation (e.g., a high percentage in stocks) will offer higher growth potential but comes with more risk. A conservative allocation (e.g., a higher percentage in bonds) will offer stability but lower returns.

2. Dollar-Cost Averaging (DCA):

Dollar-cost averaging involves investing a fixed amount of money at regular intervals, regardless of market conditions. By doing so, you buy more shares when prices are low and fewer shares when prices are high, which can reduce the impact of market volatility.

3. Stop-Loss Orders:

A stop-loss order is an automated trade that sells a stock if its price falls to a certain level. This helps limit potential losses on individual investments and ensures you don't lose more than you're comfortable with.

4. Hedging:

Hedging involves taking an offsetting position to reduce potential losses in your portfolio. For example, if you own stocks, you might buy put options to protect against a market decline. Hedging can be complex, but it's a useful strategy for experienced investors looking to manage risk.

5. Emergency Fund:

Before making significant investments, it's essential to have an emergency fund in place. This fund should cover 3–6 months of living expenses and be kept in a liquid, low-risk account. Having an emergency fund ensures that you won't need to liquidate investments during a market downturn to cover unexpected expenses.

Balancing Risk and Return

Every investment carries some degree of risk, but the key is finding the right balance between risk and return for your individual situation. This balance is often referred to as the "risk-return tradeoff."

Risk-Return Tradeoff:

High Risk, High Return: Investments like stocks, real estate, and high-yield bonds tend to offer higher returns over time, but they also come with more volatility and risk.

Low Risk, Low Return: Investments like government bonds, CDs, and money market funds offer lower returns but come with less risk and more stability.

The goal is to find a balance that matches your financial goals, risk tolerance, and time horizon. A younger investor may opt for a higher-risk portfolio with greater potential for growth, while someone nearing retirement may prioritize preserving wealth over seeking high returns.

Evaluating and Adjusting Your Portfolio Over Time

As markets fluctuate and your financial goals evolve, it's essential to evaluate and adjust your investment portfolio periodically. The key to long-term success is not only building a diversified portfolio but also actively managing it to ensure that it aligns with your evolving needs.

When to Evaluate Your Portfolio:

Annually: At least once a year, take the time to review your portfolio. This helps ensure that your asset allocation still reflects your goals and risk tolerance. Annual reviews also give you a chance to rebalance your investments if market fluctuations have altered your desired allocation.

Life Events: Major life events such as marriage, the birth of a child, or approaching retirement may require adjustments to your investment strategy. During these times, reassess your risk tolerance and financial goals, and adjust your portfolio accordingly.

Market Conditions: While it's important not to overreact to short-term market movements, significant economic shifts or market crashes may warrant a review of your portfolio. If certain asset classes or sectors are underperforming, you might want to consider rebalancing or adjusting your exposure.

How to Rebalance Your Portfolio:

Rebalancing involves buying or selling assets to restore your original asset allocation. For example, if your target allocation is 60% stocks and 40% bonds, but a market rally causes your stocks to grow to 70%, you would sell some stocks and buy bonds to bring the portfolio back to its target balance.

When Rebalancing is Necessary:

Drift in Allocation: If your portfolio's allocation drifts more than 5-10% from its target, it's a good time to rebalance.

Changes in Risk Tolerance: As you age or your financial situation changes, your risk tolerance may shift. In such cases, you might want to adjust your allocation to reflect a more conservative or aggressive approach.

Psychological Aspects of Investing

Investing isn't just a numbers game—it also involves managing your emotions and avoiding common psychological pitfalls. Even with a well-diversified portfolio, it's easy to make mistakes when emotions cloud your judgment. Understanding these psychological factors can help you avoid making irrational decisions during market highs or lows.

Common Behavioral Biases:

Herd Mentality: This occurs when investors follow the crowd, buying into assets that are popular without doing proper research. This behavior can lead to overvaluation and potential losses when market bubbles burst.

Loss Aversion: Investors tend to feel the pain of losses more acutely than the pleasure of gains, leading to irrational decisions such as selling off assets during downturns to avoid further losses. However, markets tend to recover over time, and panic selling can lock in losses.

Overconfidence: Believing you can consistently predict market movements can lead to taking on too much risk. Even experienced investors can fall into this trap, which can lead to poor decisions and underperformance.

Anchoring: Anchoring is the tendency to rely too heavily on the first piece of information encountered. For example, if you buy a stock at $100, you might focus too much on that price as an anchor, even if the stock's fundamentals change drastically.

How to Overcome Emotional Investing:

Stick to Your Plan: Create an investment plan based on your goals and risk tolerance, and stick to it even when emotions run high. Avoid making knee-jerk reactions during market volatility.

Focus on the Long Term: The stock market and other investments can be volatile in the short term, but history has shown that long-term investors are more likely to succeed. Keep your focus on the long-term growth of your portfolio.

Dollar-Cost Averaging: By regularly investing the same amount regardless of market conditions, dollar-cost averaging can help mitigate emotional decision-making, as you're consistently investing over time.

Protecting Against Black Swan Events

Black swan events are rare, unpredictable occurrences that can have severe consequences on the markets and economy. Examples include financial crises, global pandemics, and political upheaval. While these events are difficult to foresee, there are ways to protect your portfolio from extreme market shocks.

Strategies to Protect Against Black Swan Events:

Diversify Across Asset Classes: Having a well-diversified portfolio across asset classes such as stocks, bonds, real estate, and commodities can help cushion the blow of a black swan event. Different asset classes tend to react differently to market shocks, offering some level of protection.

Hold Cash Reserves: Keeping a portion of your portfolio in cash or cash equivalents (e.g., money market funds, short-term bonds) can provide liquidity during a crisis. Cash reserves also allow you to take advantage of buying opportunities when markets are down.

Invest in Defensive Assets: Defensive assets, such as gold or bonds, tend to perform well during periods of market stress. Allocating a portion of your portfolio to these types of investments can help mitigate losses during market downturns.

Consider Hedging: Hedging involves using financial instruments like options or inverse ETFs to protect against potential losses. While not necessary for all investors, sophisticated investors may use these tools to manage downside risk.

The Role of Passive vs. Active Investing in Risk Management

When managing risk in your investment portfolio, one of the key decisions is whether to take an active or passive approach. Both strategies have their advantages and drawbacks, and the right choice depends on your individual goals, risk tolerance, and time commitment.

Active Investing:

Active investing involves actively managing a portfolio by selecting specific stocks, bonds, or other assets in an attempt to outperform the market. Active investors rely on research, analysis, and market timing to make investment decisions.

Pros: Potential for higher returns if the investor can consistently identify outperforming assets. Active investors can adjust their portfolios based on market conditions.

Cons: Active investing requires significant time, expertise, and research. It also comes with higher costs due to management fees and trading expenses. Additionally, even professional active investors often struggle to consistently beat the market.

Passive Investing:

Passive investing involves buying and holding a broad range of assets through index funds or ETFs, with the goal of matching market returns rather than outperforming them. The strategy focuses on long-term growth and minimizing costs.

Pros: Lower fees and costs, less time-intensive, and typically more stable over the long term. Passive investing takes advantage of market efficiency and compounding returns over time.

Cons: No potential to outperform the market. During periods of high volatility, passive investors may experience the same downturn as the market without the flexibility to adjust their holdings.

Which Strategy is Right for You?

For most investors, a combination of both active and passive strategies can be effective. Passive investing is a great foundation for long-term wealth building, while active investing may be suitable for those with a strong understanding of the market and a desire to take a more hands-on approach.

Conclusion:

In this lesson, we've covered a wide range of strategies for diversification and risk management, each essential for creating a robust investment portfolio that can withstand market volatility while aiming for long-term growth. The goal of risk management is not to eliminate risk—this is impossible in investing—but to ensure that the risks you take are calculated, manageable, and aligned with your overall financial goals.

Here are the key takeaways:

Diversification is your best defense against market volatility. By spreading your investments across asset classes, sectors, and geographic regions, you reduce your exposure to any single risk.

Risk management involves strategies like dollar-cost averaging, stop-loss orders, and hedging to protect your portfolio from significant downturns.

Rebalancing your portfolio regularly ensures that your asset allocation remains aligned with your goals and risk tolerance.

Emotional discipline is crucial. Avoid reacting to short-term market movements, and stay focused on your long-term plan.

While black swan events are unpredictable, maintaining a diversified portfolio and holding some defensive assets can provide protection during times of crisis.

As you continue your journey toward financial independence, always remember that investing is a marathon, not a sprint. Long-term growth and wealth preservation require careful planning, disciplined execution, and a strong understanding of both the risks and opportunities present in the market.

This completes Module 3: Investing for Long-Term Growth. Up next is Module 4: Passive Income and Wealth Preservation, where we'll dive deeper into strategies for generating consistent passive income streams and protecting your accumulated wealth for the long haul. Stay tuned!

Module 4: Passive Income Strategies

In Module 4, we explore how to build sustainable streams of passive income, providing a foundation for financial independence. The key to successful passive income lies in understanding the various strategies available, how they work, and which ones align best with your goals and resources. This module covers different approaches to creating passive income, anging from traditional investments like stocks and real estate to more modern strategies like selling digital products.

Lesson Breakdown

Lesson 1: Introduction to Passive Income

Overview of Passive Income: What passive income is, why it's important, and how it differs from earned income.
Benefits of Passive Income: Achieving financial freedom, stability, and time flexibility.
Types of Passive Income: Dividend investing, real estate, digital products, affiliate marketing, royalties, and more.
Steps to Build Passive Income: Setting goals, identifying opportunities, investing time or money, automation, and scaling.

Lesson 2: Dividend Investing

Understanding Dividends: Learn how dividends work, the types of companies that pay dividends, and the benefits of dividend investing.
Building a Dividend Portfolio: Step-by-step guidance on selecting the right dividend-paying stocks, reinvesting dividends, and growing your portfolio.
Dividend Yield and Dividend Growth: Key metrics to consider when evaluating dividend stocks.
Dividend Reinvestment Plans (DRIPs): How to automatically reinvest dividends and compound your earnings over time.

Lesson 3: Rental Property Ownership

Introduction to Real Estate Investing: Explore the benefits of real estate for generating passive income, including appreciation and tax advantages.
Finding and Financing Rental Properties: Steps for identifying profitable rental properties, securing financing, and calculating returns.
Managing Rental Properties: Learn about property management options, handling tenants, and minimizing vacancies.
Passive Income from Rental Properties: How to turn rental properties into a reliable stream of passive income.

Lesson 4: Creating and Selling Digital Products

Why Digital Products?: The rise of the digital economy and why digital products like e-books, courses, and software are ideal for passive income.

Creating a Successful Digital Product: How to identify a profitable niche, create high-quality content, and launch your product.

Selling Digital Products Online: Platforms and strategies for marketing and selling your digital products to a global audience.

Scaling Your Digital Product Business: Automating sales, building funnels, and increasing revenue over time.

Conclusion of Module 4: By the end of this module, you will understand various passive income strategies and be equipped with the tools to start building your own income streams. From dividend investing to rental properties and digital products, the knowledge gained in this module will set you on the path to financial independence and long-term wealth creation.

Lesson 1: Introduction to Passive Income

1. The Mindset for Creating Passive Income

To successfully build passive income, it's crucial to develop the right mindset. Generating passive income requires a long-term approach, strategic planning, and patience. Many people make the mistake of thinking that passive income is an easy way to get rich quickly. In reality, it takes time, effort, and often money upfront. However, once established, passive income streams can grow exponentially and provide lasting financial rewards.

Key Aspects of the Passive Income Mindset:

Delayed Gratification: Passive income streams often take time to develop and may not generate substantial earnings immediately. You must be prepared to invest time and resources upfront, knowing the real payoff comes later.

Consistency and Patience: Building a reliable source of passive income involves consistency. Whether it's adding to your investment portfolio regularly or continually optimizing a digital product for better sales, it's essential to remain patient and focused on the long term.

Leveraging Time and Money: Passive income is about making your money or efforts work for you over time. This requires a shift in thinking from active earning, where you trade time for money, to leveraging systems that generate income with minimal ongoing involvement.

Diversification of Income Streams: A key component of passive income success is diversification. Relying on one source of passive income can be risky. By developing multiple streams of income, you can protect yourself from market fluctuations, economic downturns, or changes in your primary source of revenue.

2. Passive Income vs. Active Income: Why Focus on Passive?

Most people are accustomed to earning active income, which involves trading time for money—whether it's through a traditional job, freelancing, or providing a service. While active income is essential, it has limits. You can only work so many hours in a day, and there's often a ceiling to how much you can earn. This is where passive income becomes incredibly powerful.

Key Differences:

Active Income: Requires continuous work and effort to maintain. If you stop working, the income stops.

Passive Income: Requires initial effort or investment but generates revenue with minimal ongoing work. Once the system is set up, it continues to earn money over time.

The Power of Compound Growth: One of the most attractive aspects of passive income is the potential for compounding returns, especially when it comes to investing. For example, dividend stocks or interest-bearing assets grow your wealth by reinvesting earnings, which then generate more income, creating a snowball effect over time. Similarly, in real estate, rental income can be reinvested into new properties, further increasing your earnings potential.

Time Freedom: Passive income can provide you with time freedom—something active income rarely offers. Once your passive income streams are set up, you can earn money while traveling, sleeping, or pursuing other ventures. This time freedom allows you to focus on things you love, whether that's building new income streams, spending time with family, or exploring personal passions.

3. The Most Common Types of Passive Income

Dividend Investing: This involves investing in companies that distribute a portion of their profits to shareholders in the form of dividends. Dividend-paying stocks can provide a steady stream of passive income over time, especially if you reinvest dividends to buy more shares. Over time, this reinvestment leads to compounded growth.

Advantages:

Reliable income stream (especially with blue-chip companies).

Potential for capital appreciation in addition to dividends.

Tax advantages in certain countries.

Disadvantages:

Dividend payments can fluctuate based on the company's profitability.

Requires significant initial capital to generate substantial income.

Real Estate Investments: Real estate is one of the most popular passive income vehicles. Whether you're investing in rental properties, REITs (Real Estate Investment Trusts), or crowdfunding platforms, real estate can provide long-term returns and appreciation.

Advantages:

Steady monthly income from rent.

Property value appreciation over time.

Tax benefits such as deductions for property maintenance.

Disadvantages:

Requires significant upfront investment.

Property management can be time-consuming unless outsourced.

Market volatility and vacancy risks.

Digital Products: In the digital age, creating and selling digital products—such as e-books, online courses, or software—is a powerful passive income strategy. The beauty of digital products is that they can be created once and sold repeatedly to a global audience with minimal ongoing effort.

Advantages:

High-profit margins.

Scalability (no limit to the number of sales you can make).

Can be automated (through digital platforms like Amazon, Udemy, or Shopify).

Disadvantages:

Requires upfront effort to create high-quality products.

Market competition can be intense.

Marketing and promoting your product require an initial time commitment.

Affiliate Marketing: Affiliate marketing is a strategy where you promote other companies' products and earn a commission for every sale made through your referral link. This form of income is attractive because it requires little upfront investment and can be a great way to monetize a blog, YouTube channel, or social media following.

Advantages:

Low upfront cost.

No need to create your own product.

Can generate recurring income with evergreen content.

Disadvantages:

Income depends on traffic to your content.

Commissions can be small unless promoting high-ticket items.

Requires ongoing content creation to sustain earnings.

Peer-to-Peer Lending: Peer-to-peer lending platforms like LendingClub or Prosper allow you to lend money to individuals or small businesses in exchange for interest payments. While this can be riskier than other forms of passive income, it offers higher potential returns.

> **Advantages:**
>
> Higher returns than traditional savings accounts or bonds.
>
> Flexibility to lend small amounts.
>
> **Disadvantages:**
>
> Risk of borrower default.
>
> Income is not guaranteed, and principal could be lost.

4. Challenges of Building Passive Income

While passive income offers a path to financial freedom, there are challenges to consider:

Upfront Effort or Capital: Building passive income requires either significant time and effort (like creating digital products) or financial resources (like buying rental properties). It's essential to be prepared for this initial phase.

Risk: Many passive income strategies involve risk. Whether it's the risk of tenant vacancies in real estate or market downturns in dividend investing, you must account for uncertainties and create strategies to mitigate risks.

Maintenance: Although passive income is designed to run with minimal effort, some level of maintenance is often required. For instance, real estate requires property management, and digital products may need updates or ongoing marketing.

5. How to Get Started with Passive Income

Building passive income streams starts with understanding your goals, risk tolerance, and resources. Here's a roadmap to guide you:

Step 1: Assess Your Current Financial Situation:

Take a close look at your current finances. How much can you invest? Do you have time to create a digital product? Your starting point will help determine which passive income strategy makes the most sense for you.

Step 2: Choose the Right Passive Income Stream for You:

Depending on your resources, skills, and interests, choose a passive income strategy that aligns with your goals. For example, if you have capital to invest, you might consider real estate or dividend stocks. If you have skills in a particular area, creating a digital product could be more suitable.

Step 3: Take Action and Start Building:

Once you've decided on a strategy, start building. If you're creating a digital product, spend time on high-quality content creation. If you're investing in dividend stocks, research companies with strong dividend histories and stable growth.

Step 4: Automate and Optimize:

The key to passive income is automation. Whether it's setting up automatic dividend reinvestments, automating your digital product sales funnel, or hiring a property management company, find ways to reduce your ongoing involvement.

Step 5: Scale Your Income Streams:

Once you've established your first passive income stream, look for ways to scale it or diversify into new areas. For example, if you have a successful e-book, you could turn it into an online course or invest the proceeds into dividend stocks or real estate.

Conclusion: The Power of Passive Income

Passive income is a game-changer for achieving financial independence and creating long-term wealth. By building multiple income streams, you gain more control over your financial future and free up your time to focus on what matters most to you. Remember, passive income requires upfront effort or investment, but with patience and persistence, you can enjoy the rewards for years to come. The journey starts with understanding the types of passive income available and choosing the right strategy based on your unique situation and goals.

In the next lesson, we'll dive into one of the most popular passive income strategies: Dividend Investing.

Lesson 2: Dividend Investing

In this lesson, we'll take an in-depth look at dividend investing, one of the most reliable and widely used methods for generating passive income. Dividend investing is a strategy that involves buying shares of companies that regularly distribute a portion of their earnings to shareholders in the form of dividends. By building a portfolio of dividend-paying stocks, you can create a steady stream of income, often with the potential for growth through reinvestment.

This lesson will cover:

What dividends are and how they work

The benefits of dividend investing

Key metrics for evaluating dividend stocks

How to build and maintain a dividend portfolio

Dividend reinvestment plans (DRIPs)

1. Understanding Dividends

What are Dividends?

Dividends are payments made by a company to its shareholders, typically in the form of cash, but sometimes in the form of additional shares. These payments are usually made from the company's profits and are distributed on a regular basis, such as quarterly or annually.

Not all companies pay dividends—those that do are often established, profitable businesses with steady cash flows. Dividends are a way for these companies to share their success with their investors.

Types of Dividends:

Cash Dividends: The most common form, paid directly to shareholders as cash.

Stock Dividends: Instead of cash, shareholders receive additional shares of the company.

Special Dividends: One-time payments made when a company has a particularly profitable year.

How Dividends Are Paid:

Most companies pay dividends on a quarterly basis, but some may choose to pay monthly, semi-annually, or annually. When a company declares a dividend, they announce a record date, which is the cutoff for who is eligible to receive the dividend. To receive the dividend, you must own the stock before the ex-dividend date, which is typically a few days before the record date.

2. Benefits of Dividend Investing

Reliable Income Stream: Dividend-paying stocks provide a consistent income stream, which can be especially useful for retirees or anyone looking to supplement their earned income. Dividends tend to be more stable than stock prices, which can fluctuate due to market conditions.

Dividend Reinvestment: A powerful feature of dividend investing is the ability to reinvest dividends through Dividend Reinvestment Plans (DRIPs). These plans automatically use the cash dividends you receive to purchase additional shares of the company, allowing your investment to grow through compounding over time.

Potential for Capital Appreciation: In addition to the income from dividends, you can also benefit from the stock price appreciating over time. This combination of income and growth makes dividend-paying stocks a valuable addition to a long-term investment portfolio.

Hedge Against Inflation: Historically, companies that pay dividends tend to increase their dividends over time, helping investors keep up with inflation. As the cost of living rises, dividend increases can provide higher income to offset inflationary pressures.

Tax Advantages: In many countries, dividends are taxed at a lower rate than regular income. For example, in the United States, qualified dividends are taxed at the long-term capital gains rate, which can be lower than the rate on ordinary income. This makes dividend investing a tax-efficient strategy for building wealth.

3. Key Metrics for Evaluating Dividend Stocks

When investing in dividend-paying companies, it's essential to look beyond the dividend yield and consider several key factors to ensure you're investing in financially stable businesses. Below are some of the most important metrics to evaluate:

Dividend Yield: This is the annual dividend payment divided by the stock price, expressed as a percentage. While a high dividend yield might seem attractive, it can sometimes signal that the company is struggling, and the stock price has fallen as a result. A good rule of thumb is to aim for stocks with moderate, sustainable yields rather than chasing the highest yields.

Formula:

Dividend Yield=Annual Dividend Payment/Stock Price Price

Payout Ratio: The payout ratio shows the percentage of earnings that a company is paying out as dividends. A lower payout ratio (typically below 60%) suggests that the company is retaining enough of its earnings to reinvest in growth, while still rewarding shareholders. A very high payout ratio could indicate that the company is paying out most of its profits as dividends, which may not be sustainable in the long term.

Formula:

Payout Ratio=(Dividends per Share/Earnings per Share)×100

Dividend Growth: Look for companies with a track record of growing their dividends over time. Companies that consistently increase their dividends signal financial strength and management's confidence in future earnings. The Dividend Growth Rate (DGR) indicates how much a company's dividend has grown annually over a certain period.

Free Cash Flow (FCF): This metric represents the cash a company generates after accounting for capital expenditures. A company with strong free cash flow is more likely to sustain or increase its dividend payments.

Dividend Coverage Ratio: This measures the company's ability to pay its dividends from its earnings. A ratio of 2 or higher suggests the company is comfortably able to pay its dividends from profits, leaving room for reinvestment and growth.

4. Building and Maintaining a Dividend Portfolio

Building a successful dividend portfolio requires diversification, regular monitoring, and a focus on long-term growth. Here's how to get started:

Choose Dividend-Paying Stocks: Look for companies with a history of paying and increasing dividends. Some of the best choices are Dividend Aristocrats—companies that have consistently raised their dividends for at least 25 consecutive years.

Diversify Across Sectors: Diversification is crucial to managing risk. Don't concentrate all your investments in one industry. For example, utilities and consumer staples are known for steady dividends, but you should also consider dividend-paying stocks from sectors like technology, healthcare, and financials to spread risk.

Reinvest Dividends: If your goal is long-term wealth building, reinvesting dividends is one of the best ways to grow your portfolio. With DRIPs, your dividends are automatically reinvested to purchase more shares, which then generate their own dividends, creating a compounding effect.

Monitor Your Investments: Regularly review your dividend portfolio to ensure the companies you've invested in are still financially sound. While you want to hold dividend stocks for the long term, you should also be prepared to make adjustments if a company's financial health declines or if there are better opportunities elsewhere.

Set Up an Emergency Fund: Though dividends are a relatively stable form of income, they're not guaranteed, especially in times of economic downturn. Setting up an emergency fund ensures that you won't need to rely solely on dividend income during periods of market volatility.

5. Dividend Reinvestment Plans (DRIPs)

Dividend Reinvestment Plans (DRIPs) are an essential tool for any dividend investor looking to maximize their returns through compounding. With a DRIP, you automatically reinvest your dividends to purchase additional shares of the stock instead of receiving cash. This strategy helps your investment grow more quickly by using the power of compounding.

Advantages of DRIPs:

Automatic Reinvestment: DRIPs allow you to reinvest dividends without having to pay brokerage fees, allowing you to accumulate more shares over time.

Compounding Growth: Each additional share purchased through a DRIP generates its own dividends, accelerating the compounding effect.

Fractional Shares: DRIPs often allow you to purchase fractional shares, so you're always reinvesting the full dividend amount, even if it's less than the cost of a full share.

Conclusion: The Power of Dividend Investing

Dividend investing is one of the most powerful and reliable ways to generate passive income. With a well-constructed portfolio of dividend-paying stocks, you can enjoy consistent income while also benefiting from capital appreciation over time. The keys to success in dividend investing are careful stock selection, focusing on long-term growth, and reinvesting dividends to maximize the power of compounding.

In the next lesson, we'll explore another popular passive income strategy: Real Estate Investment for Passive Income.

Lesson 3: Real Estate Investment Strategies

Real estate is one of the most time-tested methods of building wealth and generating passive income. From rental properties to real estate investment trusts (REITs), real estate offers several avenues for consistent income, asset appreciation, and portfolio diversification. In this lesson, we'll explore the various strategies for investing in real estate, the pros and cons of each, and how to get started.

This lesson will cover:

Why invest in real estate?

Rental properties: buy, hold, and rent

Real estate investment trusts (REITs)

Real estate crowdfunding platforms

Key factors to consider before investing in real estate

How to get started in real estate investing

1. Why Invest in Real Estate?

Real estate has long been considered a stable and profitable investment, offering both passive income and the potential for long-term wealth accumulation. Here are some of the top reasons to consider real estate as part of your wealth-building strategy:

Steady Cash Flow: One of the main advantages of real estate is the ability to generate a steady cash flow through rental income. A well-chosen property can provide consistent monthly income, which can either supplement your active earnings or replace it entirely once you've built up a large enough portfolio.

Appreciation Over Time: Real estate tends to appreciate in value over time, especially in growing markets. This means that in addition to earning rental income, you can also benefit from the property's value increasing over the years.

Tax Benefits: Real estate investors often enjoy significant tax benefits, including deductions for property taxes, mortgage interest, and depreciation. These tax advantages can reduce your overall tax liability and enhance your returns.

Leverage: Real estate allows you to leverage other people's money—typically through mortgage financing—to purchase an asset that appreciates and generates income. This means you can control a valuable asset with a relatively small initial investment.

Hedge Against Inflation: As inflation rises, the value of real estate typically increases as well, making it a good hedge against inflation. Additionally, rental income tends to rise over time, allowing you to keep pace with the cost of living.

2. Rental Properties: Buy, Hold, and Rent

Owning rental properties is one of the most common and direct ways to invest in real estate. This strategy involves buying a property, holding onto it, and renting it out to generate monthly income. There are two primary types of rental properties: residential and commercial.

Residential Rental Properties: These include single-family homes, duplexes, townhouses, or apartments that are rented to individual tenants. Residential properties are often easier to finance and manage than commercial properties, making them a popular choice for beginner real estate investors.

Commercial Rental Properties: These include office buildings, retail spaces, warehouses, and industrial properties that are rented to businesses. Commercial properties can offer higher rental income and longer lease terms but tend to require more capital and expertise to manage.

Pros of Rental Properties:

Steady cash flow from rental income.

Potential for appreciation in property value over time.

Tax benefits, including deductions for depreciation, interest, and repairs.

Ability to leverage financing to increase your returns.

Cons of Rental Properties:

Property management can be time-consuming, especially with problem tenants.

Risk of vacancies or tenants defaulting on rent.

High upfront costs for down payments, repairs, and maintenance.

Property market fluctuations can affect the value of the asset.

How to Choose a Rental Property:

Location: The location of the property is one of the most critical factors in its success. Look for areas with strong job markets, good schools, and growing populations.

Cash Flow Potential: Calculate the potential rental income and subtract expenses such as mortgage payments, property taxes, insurance, and maintenance to determine whether the property will generate positive cash flow.

Condition of the Property: Older properties may need more repairs and maintenance, which can eat into your profits. Ensure you have a thorough inspection before purchasing.

Financing Options: Shop around for the best mortgage rates and loan terms. Consider how much leverage you're comfortable with and how it will affect your returns.

3. Real Estate Investment Trusts (REITs)

If you're interested in real estate but don't want the hassle of managing physical properties, Real Estate Investment Trusts (REITs) offer a great alternative. REITs are companies that own, operate, or finance income-producing real estate across a range of sectors, including residential, commercial, industrial, and healthcare properties. By purchasing shares of a REIT, you can invest in real estate without having to buy or manage property directly.

Types of REITs:

Equity REITs: These REITs own and operate income-producing real estate. They generate income primarily from renting out properties and distributing a portion of the rental income to shareholders.

Mortgage REITs: These REITs invest in real estate debt, such as mortgages or mortgage-backed securities. They earn income from the interest on these loans.

Hybrid REITs: These REITs combine both equity and mortgage investments.

Pros of Investing in REITs:

Liquidity: Unlike physical properties, REITs are traded on stock exchanges, making them highly liquid. You can buy or sell shares easily, just like stocks.

Diversification: REITs provide exposure to a broad range of properties and real estate sectors, offering diversification within the real estate market.

Income: REITs are required to distribute at least 90% of their taxable income to shareholders in the form of dividends, making them a reliable source of passive income.

Low Barriers to Entry: You can start investing in REITs with a relatively small amount of capital compared to purchasing a property.

Cons of Investing in REITs:

Market Volatility: Since REITs are traded on stock exchanges, their prices can fluctuate with the broader market, even though they are based on real estate assets.

Dividend Taxation: REIT dividends are often taxed at ordinary income rates, which can be higher than the rates for qualified dividends or capital gains.

Management Fees: Some REITs charge management fees, which can eat into your returns over time.

4. Real Estate Crowdfunding Platforms

For investors who want to pool their money with others to invest in real estate, crowdfunding platforms offer a compelling option. These platforms allow you to invest in a range of real estate projects, from residential developments to commercial properties, often with a lower capital requirement than purchasing a property outright.

How Real Estate Crowdfunding Works: Crowdfunding platforms typically allow you to browse different real estate projects and choose which ones to invest in. You can often invest with as little as $500 or $1,000, depending on the platform. The platform then pools your money with other investors to fund the real estate project.

Pros of Real Estate Crowdfunding:

Lower Capital Requirements: Crowdfunding platforms allow you to invest in real estate with much less capital than traditional property investments.

Diversification: You can invest in multiple projects across different markets, reducing your risk exposure.

Passive Income: Similar to REITs, crowdfunding investments generate passive income from rental payments or property appreciation.

Cons of Real Estate Crowdfunding:

Liquidity Issues: Real estate crowdfunding investments are often illiquid, meaning your money could be tied up for several years until the project is completed or sold.

Platform Fees: Crowdfunding platforms typically charge fees, which can reduce your overall returns.

Risk: As with any real estate investment, there is a risk that the project may not generate the expected returns, or worse, you could lose your entire investment if the project fails.

5. Key Factors to Consider Before Investing in Real Estate

Before diving into real estate investing, there are several key factors to consider to ensure you're making the right decision:

Market Research: Research local real estate markets to identify areas with strong rental demand, property appreciation potential, and economic growth. Understanding market trends is crucial to making a successful investment.

Financing and Leverage: Consider how much leverage (debt) you're willing to take on. While financing a property can amplify your returns, it also increases your risk, especially if the rental income doesn't cover your mortgage payments.

Property Management: If you don't want to manage properties yourself, consider hiring a property management company. While this will reduce your profits, it can save you time and effort, especially if you own multiple properties.

Exit Strategy: Have a clear exit strategy in place before you invest. Whether you plan to sell the property for a profit or hold onto it for long-term rental income, knowing your end goal will help guide your investment decisions.

6. How to Get Started in Real Estate Investing

Starting in real estate doesn't have to be overwhelming. Here are some steps to get you going:

Step 1: Define Your Goals: Decide what you want to achieve with real estate investing. Are you looking for steady cash flow, long-term appreciation, or both? Your goals will influence the type of real estate you invest in.

Step 2: Research and Educate Yourself: Take the time to learn about different real estate investment strategies and the markets you're interested in. There are many resources available, including books, online courses, and real estate investment groups.

Step 3: Secure Financing: Determine how much capital you can invest and explore financing options. Speak with lenders to understand the terms and rates available to you.

Step 4: Start Small: Consider starting with a small property or a REIT investment to get a feel for real estate investing. As you gain experience and build your portfolio, you can move on to larger or more complex investments.

Step 5: Build a Network: Real estate investing is often a team effort. Build relationships with real estate agents, lenders, contractors, and property managers who can help you succeed.

Conclusion: The Long-Term Value of Real Estate

Real estate offers numerous opportunities to generate passive income and build long-term wealth. Whether you choose to invest in rental properties, REITs, or crowdfunding platforms, real estate can be a powerful addition to your wealth-building strategy. By understanding the risks, conducting thorough research, and taking a patient, long-term approach, you can unlock the financial benefits of real estate investing.

In the next lesson, we'll explore the final passive income strategy: Creating and Selling Digital Products.

Next Lesson: Creating and Selling Digital Products

Lesson 4: Creating and Selling Digital Products

Digital products are a fantastic way to generate passive income. They require an upfront investment of time and effort to create, but once they're made, they can be sold repeatedly with little additional work. In this lesson, we'll explore the various types of digital products you can create, the steps to develop and market them, and strategies to maximize your income.

This lesson will cover:

Understanding digital products

Types of digital products

Steps to create a digital product

Marketing and selling your digital product

Maximizing your passive income

1. Understanding Digital Products

Digital products are intangible goods that can be sold and delivered online. Unlike physical products, they don't require inventory, shipping, or storage. This makes them an attractive option for entrepreneurs and creators looking to build a sustainable passive income stream.

Benefits of Digital Products:

Low Overhead Costs: Once created, digital products incur minimal costs for distribution and delivery.

Scalability: You can sell an unlimited number of copies without additional production costs.

Global Reach: Digital products can be sold to customers around the world, increasing your potential market.

Automated Sales: With the right systems in place, you can automate sales and delivery, allowing you to earn income passively.

2. Types of Digital Products

There are many types of digital products you can create, each with its unique market potential. Here are some popular options:

E-books: E-books are electronic versions of books that can be downloaded and read on various devices. Topics can range from fiction to self-help, business, and personal development. E-books are relatively easy to create and can be marketed on platforms like Amazon Kindle Direct Publishing.

Online Courses: Creating an online course is a powerful way to share your knowledge and expertise. You can use platforms like Udemy, Teachable, or your own website to host and sell your course. Courses can include video lectures, quizzes, and downloadable resources.

Digital Templates and Planners: Templates and planners are highly sought after by individuals and businesses looking for organization and efficiency. Examples include budget planners, social media templates, and website themes. They can be sold through platforms like Etsy or your website.

Stock Photos and Graphics: If you're a photographer or graphic designer, you can create and sell stock photos, illustrations, and design elements. Websites like Shutterstock, Adobe Stock, and Creative Market allow you to upload and sell your work to a global audience.

Software and Apps: If you have programming skills, consider creating software applications or mobile apps. These can solve specific problems or offer unique functionalities, and they can be sold through app stores or as downloadable software on your website.

Music and Audio Files: Musicians and sound designers can sell their music, sound effects, or audio courses. Platforms like SoundCloud, Bandcamp, or even your website can be used to market your audio products.

3. Steps to Create a Digital Product

Creating a digital product involves several key steps. Here's a breakdown of the process:

Step 1: Identify Your Niche:

Choose a niche that aligns with your expertise and interests. Research market demand and competition to ensure there's a viable audience for your product.

Step 2: Validate Your Idea:

Before investing significant time into development, validate your product idea by conducting surveys, joining relevant online communities, or pre-selling your product. This will help ensure that there is interest in your product.

Step 3: Develop Your Product:

Create your digital product using high-quality tools and resources. Here are some tips for different types of products:

E-books: Use software like Microsoft Word or Scrivener for writing, and design tools like Canva or Adobe InDesign for layout and design.

Online Courses: Use video editing software to create high-quality video content, and consider using platforms like PowerPoint for presentations.

Templates: Design your templates using tools like Canva, Adobe Illustrator, or Google Docs.

Software: Follow software development best practices and consider collaborating with a developer if needed.

Step 4: Create a Sales Funnel:

Set up a sales funnel that guides potential customers from awareness to purchase. This can include a landing page, email marketing, and social media promotion. Use persuasive copy and compelling visuals to attract buyers.

Step 5: Pricing Your Product:

Determine a fair price for your product based on its value, the market rate, and your target audience. Consider offering tiered pricing or discounts for early buyers to encourage initial sales.

4. Marketing and Selling Your Digital Product

Once you've created your digital product, it's time to market and sell it. Here are some strategies to effectively promote your product:

Build an Online Presence: Establish a website or blog where you can share valuable content related to your niche. This will help build credibility and attract potential customers. Use SEO strategies to optimize your content for search engines.

Utilize Social Media: Leverage social media platforms like Instagram, Facebook, Twitter, and LinkedIn to reach your audience. Create engaging content that showcases your product and encourages sharing.

Content Marketing: Write blog posts, create videos, or host webinars that provide value to your audience while subtly promoting your product. Content marketing can position you as an authority in your niche.

Email Marketing: Build an email list of potential customers and send regular newsletters with updates, tips, and promotions related to your product. Email marketing has one of the highest ROI among marketing channels.

Collaborate with Influencers: Partner with influencers or bloggers in your niche who can help promote your product to their audience. This can expand your reach and build credibility.

Utilize Online Marketplaces: Consider selling your digital product on established marketplaces like Amazon, Etsy, Udemy, or Shopify. These platforms often have built-in audiences and marketing tools to help you get started.

5. Maximizing Your Passive Income

After your digital product is launched, there are several strategies you can use to maximize your passive income:

Upselling and Cross-Selling: Once you have customers, offer them additional products or services related to their original purchase. This could be a more advanced course, a bundle of templates, or a subscription service.

Create a Membership Site: Consider turning your digital products into a membership site where users pay a monthly or yearly fee for access to exclusive content, products, or community features.

Continuously Improve Your Product: Gather feedback from customers and make improvements to your product based on their input. Regular updates can keep your product relevant and encourage repeat purchases.

Diversify Your Offerings: Expand your product line by creating additional digital products. This could include new e-books, courses, or templates that complement your existing offerings.

Automate Your Sales: Set up automated systems for sales and delivery to ensure you're making money even while you sleep. This can include using email marketing automation and online payment systems.

Conclusion: The Power of Digital Products

Creating and selling digital products can be a lucrative way to build passive income. With the right approach, you can leverage your knowledge and skills to develop products that provide value to your audience while generating revenue for yourself.

As you dive into the world of digital products, remember to stay focused on delivering quality and value, continuously improve your offerings, and adapt to changing market trends. By doing so, you'll be well on your way to establishing a successful stream of passive income.

In the next module, we'll wrap up the course by discussing how to create a sustainable wealth-building plan that incorporates the various income strategies we've explored.

Module 5: Integrating Wealth Strategies into a Cohesive Financial Plan

In this module, we will focus on how to bring together all the strategies you've learned throughout the previous modules and integrate them into a comprehensive financial plan. Building wealth is not just about individual strategies but about managing them collectively in a structured, intentional way. A cohesive financial plan helps ensure your efforts align with your long-term financial goals, balancing risk and reward while adapting to changing circumstances.

In this module, we'll cover:

Assessing Your Current Financial Situation

Setting Clear Financial Goals

Building a Budget That Supports Wealth-Building

Managing Risk and Protecting Your Wealth

Creating a Long-Term Wealth Management Plan

1. Assessing Your Current Financial Situation

The first step toward creating a cohesive financial plan is understanding your current financial status. Before you can plan for the future, it's essential to have a clear picture of where you stand today.

Steps to Assess Your Financial Situation:

Step 1: Track Your Income and Expenses

List all sources of income, including salary, freelance work, side hustles, and passive income streams.

Track your monthly expenses, including both fixed expenses (e.g., rent, utilities) and variable expenses (e.g., groceries, entertainment).

Step 2: Calculate Your Net Worth

Your net worth is the difference between your assets and liabilities. It's a key metric for tracking your wealth-building progress.

Assets: This includes savings, investments (stocks, real estate, retirement accounts), and valuable possessions.

Liabilities: This includes debt such as student loans, mortgages, credit card debt, and other outstanding obligations.

Step 3: Review Your Debt

Assess the types of debt you have and their interest rates. Understanding your debt will help you prioritize which to pay off first and how to balance debt repayment with wealth-building efforts.

2. Setting Clear Financial Goals

A financial plan is only effective if you have clear, actionable goals to work toward. Financial goals can range from paying off debt to saving for retirement, building passive income streams, or purchasing a home. When setting your goals, think about both short-term and long-term objectives.

How to Set SMART Financial Goals:

Specific: Be precise about what you want to achieve (e.g., "Save $20,000 for a down payment on a house").

Measurable: Ensure your goal has clear metrics to track your progress (e.g., "Save $500 per month").

Achievable: Set realistic goals based on your current financial situation and income.

Relevant: Make sure the goal aligns with your long-term financial vision.

Time-Bound: Set a deadline for achieving your goal (e.g., "Save $20,000 in 3 years").

Common Financial Goals:

Pay off high-interest debt

Build an emergency fund (3-6 months of living expenses)

Invest in retirement accounts (401(k), IRA, etc.)

Create passive income streams through investments or business ventures

Save for significant life events (buying a home, education, travel)

3. Building a Budget That Supports Wealth-Building

Budgeting is the backbone of any financial plan. It's how you control your money and ensure you're allocating resources toward your financial goals. A wealth-building budget helps you balance living expenses with saving, investing, and paying off debt.

Steps to Create a Wealth-Building Budget:

Step 1: Prioritize Essentials

Start by covering your essential living expenses (e.g., housing, utilities, groceries, transportation). These are non-negotiable and need to be accounted for first.

Step 2: Allocate for Debt Repayment

If you have high-interest debt, prioritize paying it off as quickly as possible. Include it as a line item in your budget, focusing on paying more than the minimum to reduce overall interest costs.

Step 3: Automate Savings and Investments

Treat saving and investing as fixed expenses. Set up automatic transfers to your savings accounts, retirement accounts, or investment portfolios to ensure you consistently contribute toward building wealth.

Step 4: Track and Adjust

Track your spending regularly to ensure you're staying on track. Adjust your budget as needed to accommodate changes in income, expenses, or financial goals.

4. Managing Risk and Protecting Your Wealth

Building wealth is not just about growing your income and investments; it's also about managing risks and protecting what you've accumulated. There are several ways to mitigate financial risks and safeguard your assets.

Strategies for Managing Financial Risk:

Diversification: Diversify your investments to spread risk across different asset classes, industries, and geographical regions. This reduces the impact of any single investment loss on your overall portfolio. Invest in a mix of:

- Stocks and bonds
- Real estate
- Cash or cash equivalents
- Business ventures

Insurance: Insurance is a key component of risk management. Ensure you have adequate coverage to protect against unexpected financial losses.

Health Insurance: Protects you from high medical costs.

Life Insurance: Provides financial support for your dependents in the event of your passing.

Home and Auto Insurance: Protects your property and assets from damage or theft.

Disability Insurance: Replaces a portion of your income if you're unable to work due to illness or injury.

Emergency Fund: An emergency fund is your safety net for unexpected expenses such as medical bills, car repairs, or job loss. Having 3-6 months' worth of living expenses in a separate, easily accessible account is essential for protecting your financial stability.

Estate Planning: Creating a will or trust ensures that your assets are distributed according to your wishes and can minimize legal complications for your heirs. It's an essential part of long-term financial planning, especially as your wealth grows.

5. Creating a Long-Term Wealth Management Plan

Finally, a comprehensive financial plan should outline how you'll manage and grow your wealth over the long term. This includes strategies for continued investment, income diversification, and adjusting your plan as life circumstances change.

Key Elements of a Long-Term Wealth Management Plan:

Continued Education and Skill Development: The economy is constantly evolving, and so should your skills. Invest in education and training to stay competitive in the job market and increase your earning potential.

Diversifying Income Streams: Relying on a single source of income can be risky. Look for opportunities to diversify through side hustles, freelance work, investments, or entrepreneurship. This not only protects you from economic downturns but also accelerates wealth-building.

Periodic Review and Adjustment: Your financial goals and circumstances will change over time. Periodically review your financial plan to ensure it remains aligned with your life goals.

Reassess your budget, investments, and income sources to keep your wealth-building efforts on track.

Planning for Major Life Events: Life events such as marriage, children, buying a home, or retirement can significantly impact your financial plan. Make adjustments to accommodate these events, whether it's saving for a child's education or planning for early retirement.

Retirement Planning: Ensure that your retirement accounts are adequately funded to maintain your desired lifestyle in your later years. Maximize contributions to tax-advantaged accounts like 401(k)s and IRAs, and adjust your investment strategy as you approach retirement.

Conclusion: Building a Comprehensive Wealth Strategy

Incorporating all the strategies learned throughout this course into a cohesive financial plan is key to long-term wealth-building success. By understanding your current financial situation, setting clear goals, budgeting effectively, managing risk, and continuously adjusting your plan, you can build a solid foundation for financial freedom and wealth mastery.

The journey to wealth-building requires discipline, persistence, and a proactive approach to managing your finances. By taking control of your financial future and implementing these strategies, you'll be well on your way to achieving your wealth goals.

Module 6: Financial Independence and Early Retirement (FIRE)

The concept of Financial Independence, Retire Early (FIRE) has gained massive popularity as people strive for more control over their time and finances. FIRE is all about aggressively saving and investing to accumulate enough wealth to become financially independent, meaning you no longer have to work to cover your living expenses. In this module, we'll break down the steps to achieving financial independence and the various approaches to early retirement.

In this module, we'll cover:

What is FIRE and Why It Matters?

Types of FIRE (Lean, Fat, Barista, and Coast FIRE)

The Math Behind FIRE: Savings Rates and Investment Returns

Crafting a FIRE Plan

Life After Reaching Financial Independence

1. What is FIRE and Why It Matters?

FIRE stands for Financial Independence, Retire Early, and it focuses on the goal of saving and investing enough money to cover your living expenses without needing to work. The essence of FIRE is financial freedom—where work becomes optional, and you have the flexibility to pursue what matters most to you, whether it's traveling, hobbies, or simply having more control over your time.

The FIRE movement encourages high savings rates, minimalism, smart investing, and careful planning to reduce the time it takes to reach financial independence. While traditional retirement typically happens between ages 60-70, FIRE advocates aim for financial independence in their 30s, 40s, or 50s.

2. Types of FIRE

There are different approaches to achieving FIRE, each based on how much you want to save and the type of lifestyle you plan to maintain during retirement. Understanding these variations allows you to tailor your FIRE journey to your personal preferences and financial goals.

Lean FIRE: Lean FIRE focuses on achieving financial independence by maintaining a minimalistic lifestyle. This approach requires saving enough to cover essential living expenses while cutting out luxuries and non-essential spending. Lean FIRE is ideal for those who are willing to live frugally and enjoy a simple lifestyle.

Fat FIRE: Fat FIRE is for individuals who want to retire early but maintain a higher standard of living. This approach requires accumulating a larger retirement fund to cover more significant expenses, including luxury items, travel, and other non-essential spending. Fat FIRE is typically for people who have higher incomes and want more financial comfort in retirement.

Barista FIRE: Barista FIRE is a hybrid approach where you reach partial financial independence and then work part-time or pursue a passion project to supplement your income. This method allows for more flexibility and reduces the amount of money you need to save before you retire. Many people choose Barista FIRE because it allows them to work less while still having a safety net of savings.

Coast FIRE: Coast FIRE focuses on accumulating enough savings and investments early on so that, with compounding returns, your money will grow enough to sustain your retirement without the need for further contributions. Once you hit your "Coast FIRE" number, you can switch to a lower-stress job or pursue other interests while your investments grow passively.

3. The Math Behind FIRE: Savings Rates and Investment Returns

Achieving FIRE requires a thorough understanding of the relationship between your savings rate, investment returns, and living expenses. To reach financial independence, your investment portfolio must be large enough to cover your annual expenses indefinitely. This is often referred to as your "FIRE number."

Step 1: Calculate Your FIRE Number

Your FIRE number is the total amount of money you need to have invested to live off of your investments. A common rule of thumb used in the FIRE community is the 4% rule. This rule suggests that you can safely withdraw 4% of your portfolio annually to cover your living expenses without running out of money over a 30-year retirement.

Formula: FIRE number = (Annual living expenses) x 25

For example, if your annual living expenses are $40,000, your FIRE number would be: FIRE number = $40,000 x 25 = $1,000,000

Step 2: Determine Your Savings Rate

Your savings rate is the percentage of your income that you save and invest each year. The higher your savings rate, the faster you can reach financial independence.

For example:

If you save 10% of your income, it might take you 40+ years to retire.

If you save 50% of your income, you could potentially retire in 17-20 years.

If you save 70% of your income, you could retire in as little as 7-10 years.

Step 3: Leverage Investment Returns

Investing plays a critical role in achieving FIRE because your savings alone are unlikely to grow enough without compounding investment returns. Most FIRE adherents invest in a diversified portfolio of stocks, bonds, and other assets to generate long-term returns.

Historical stock market returns (S&P 500) have averaged about 7-8% annually after inflation. While market volatility can impact short-term gains, long-term investors benefit from compound growth over decades.

4. Crafting a FIRE Plan

Achieving FIRE requires intentional planning and discipline. To craft a FIRE plan, follow these steps:

Step 1: Track and Optimize Expenses

Start by tracking all your expenses to understand where your money is going. Cut unnecessary expenses and find ways to live more frugally without sacrificing your quality of life. Some strategies include:

Downsizing your home or moving to a lower-cost area

Using public transportation or biking instead of owning a car

Reducing entertainment and dining-out costs[1]

Step 2: Increase Your Income

While reducing expenses is crucial, increasing your income can significantly accelerate your path to FIRE. Consider:

- Negotiating for a higher salary
- Starting a side hustle or freelance work
- Investing in education or skills that will lead to higher-paying jobs

Step 3: Invest Wisely

Maximize contributions to retirement accounts (401(k), IRA) and taxable investment accounts. Consider using low-cost index funds that offer broad market exposure and lower management fees. Investing in real estate, dividend-paying stocks, or starting a business can also contribute to long-term financial independence.

Step 4: Create an Emergency Fund

Having an emergency fund ensures you won't need to dip into your investments for unexpected expenses. Aim to save 3-6 months' worth of living expenses in a high-yield savings account.

Step 5: Monitor Progress

Track your savings rate, investment returns, and overall net worth regularly. Adjust your FIRE plan as needed to account for changes in income, expenses, or life goals.

5. Life After Reaching Financial Independence

Reaching financial independence doesn't necessarily mean you have to retire early, but it gives you the freedom to choose how you spend your time. Many people who reach FIRE continue to pursue passion projects, work part-time, or travel the world.

Consider Your Post-FIRE Lifestyle

Before reaching FIRE, think about how you want to spend your time. Some common post-FIRE activities include:

- Traveling and exploring new hobbies
- Volunteering or giving back to the community
- Starting a business or working on passion projects
- Pursuing creative endeavors like writing or art

---

[1]

Financial Management in Early Retirement

Even after reaching FIRE, you need to continue managing your finances carefully. Monitor your withdrawal rates to ensure you don't outlive your savings, and adjust for changes in inflation, market returns, and your lifestyle needs.

Stay Mentally and Socially Engaged

Early retirement can lead to a loss of structure and purpose if not planned properly. Make sure you stay socially connected and mentally engaged through hobbies, activities, or part-time work that brings fulfillment.

Conclusion: Achieving Financial Independence

The journey to Financial Independence and Early Retirement (FIRE) requires commitment, discipline, and strategic planning. By combining aggressive savings, wise investments, and lifestyle optimization, FIRE gives you the freedom to live life on your own terms. Whether your goal is Lean FIRE, Fat FIRE, or something in between, the key is creating a plan that aligns with your values and financial aspirations.

By taking control of your finances and focusing on long-term wealth-building, you can achieve financial freedom and design a life that brings both fulfillment and financial security.

Sustaining FIRE: Maintaining Financial Independence Over Time

Achieving FIRE is an incredible milestone, but maintaining financial independence requires ongoing management and adaptation. Sustaining FIRE involves continuous financial vigilance, protecting against inflation, and having the flexibility to adjust to market fluctuations or changes in personal needs.

Monitoring Spending and Withdrawals

Once you've reached financial independence, managing withdrawals becomes crucial. The 4% rule is a helpful guideline, but actual withdrawal rates may vary depending on market performance, inflation, and other variables. You may need to adapt your spending habits to ensure your money lasts, especially during economic downturns.

12. **Dynamic Withdrawal Strategy**: Rather than rigidly sticking to 4%, a dynamic strategy adjusts withdrawals based on portfolio performance. This flexibility allows you to withdraw less during down markets and more during good years.

13. **Adjusting for Inflation**: Review your budget annually and adjust for inflation, ensuring that your withdrawals align with the current cost of living.

Generating Supplemental Income (If Needed)

Some people who reach FIRE prefer to have a small income stream as a cushion. This supplemental income could come from a part-time job, freelance work, or monetizing a hobby. Having extra income can help you withdraw less from your portfolio during bear markets and stretch your savings.

14. **Freelance or Remote Work**: You could take on occasional projects that align with your skills.
15. **Passive Income Streams**: Consider dividend-paying stocks, rental properties, or even digital products for a steady, low-maintenance income.

Rebalancing Your Portfolio

Once you're financially independent, regularly rebalancing your portfolio helps manage risk by maintaining your desired asset allocation. A balanced portfolio typically involves a mix of stocks, bonds, and cash that reflects your risk tolerance and income needs. Rebalancing annually ensures that your portfolio remains aligned with your goals, even as markets fluctuate.

Protecting Against Inflation and Healthcare Costs

One of the biggest challenges in early retirement is protecting against inflation and rising healthcare costs. Inflation erodes purchasing power, and healthcare can become a significant expense over time. Planning for these is essential to sustain FIRE.

16. **Inflation-Protected Investments**: Consider diversifying with Treasury Inflation-Protected Securities (TIPS) or real estate, as these assets often rise in value with inflation.
17. **Health Insurance**: Plan for healthcare by securing quality insurance, whether through the marketplace or a private insurer, and consider saving in a Health Savings Account (HSA) for medical expenses.

Staying Engaged and Purpose-Driven

Sustaining FIRE is not only about finances; it's also about emotional and mental well-being. Many people find they need a sense of purpose and connection to maintain happiness after achieving financial independence.

18. **Volunteering or Mentoring**: Giving back to your community or mentoring others in your field can offer structure and fulfillment.

19. **Hobbies and Passion Projects**: Engage in activities you've always wanted to pursue, whether it's art, writing, or travel. Living a fulfilling, purpose-driven life helps make FIRE a sustainable, enriching experience.

Conclusion: The Journey Beyond FIRE

Achieving FIRE is a remarkable accomplishment that requires strategic planning, patience, and discipline. The journey doesn't end upon reaching financial independence; rather, it opens a new chapter filled with possibilities. With the freedom to shape your life as you choose, sustaining FIRE is about careful management, flexibility, and creating a fulfilling post-FIRE life.

This module concludes our course on wealth mastery and financial independence. You've learned about budgeting, investing, passive income, and now integrating these strategies into a FIRE-based plan. Use these principles to build a life aligned with your values and goals.

Your Path to Wealth Mastery and Financial Independence

Congratulations! You've reached the final chapter in the journey to mastering wealth. This course has equipped you with the foundational and advanced strategies to build, sustain, and grow your financial independence. You've explored personal finance basics, income-boosting strategies, investing, passive income, and achieving FIRE. Now, you're empowered to create a life filled with financial security, freedom, and fulfillment.

In this final segment, we'll revisit the essential principles covered throughout the course, discuss how to apply them, and explore how you can continue evolving financially.

Reflecting on Key Takeaways

Let's revisit the core principles and strategies you've learned. Reviewing these can strengthen your commitment and solidify your path to wealth mastery:

20. **Setting Financial Goals**: Financial success starts with clear, measurable goals. Whether you aim to reduce debt, save for a large purchase, or achieve financial independence, setting goals helps guide your efforts.

21. **Income Generation**: We examined ways to increase your income through salary negotiation, freelancing, side hustles, and entrepreneurship. Higher earnings can speed up financial independence, so take time to explore and optimize your income streams.

22. **Smart Saving and Budgeting**: Essential to wealth building is understanding and controlling your cash flow. A well-planned budget, emergency fund, and high savings rate are fundamental to financial resilience and growth.

23. **Investing for Growth**: Building wealth requires investing in assets like stocks, bonds, and real estate that appreciate over time. With diversified investments, you harness the power of compounding and market returns to grow your wealth.

24. **Creating Passive Income**: From dividend investing to rental properties and digital products, we covered ways to create income streams that require minimal ongoing effort. Passive income can bring you closer to financial independence.

25. **Planning for FIRE**: Reaching Financial Independence and Early Retirement is about having the freedom to design your life on your terms. Lean, Fat, Barista, and Coast FIRE provide flexible frameworks that can match your lifestyle and savings preferences.

Building an Action Plan for Your Financial Future

To transform knowledge into lasting financial success, create a step-by-step action plan based on what you've learned:

26. **Evaluate Your Current Financial Position**: Take stock of your income, expenses, savings, and investments. Identify strengths and areas for improvement.

27. **Set Your Short and Long-Term Goals**: Define where you want to be financially in the next year, five years, and beyond. Be specific with targets—such as a certain savings amount, investment milestones, or achieving a specific FIRE goal.

28. **Select and Implement Key Strategies**: Decide which income generation, savings, investing, or passive income methods suit your lifestyle and goals. Begin with a few strategies, and expand as you gain confidence.

29. **Monitor and Adjust**: Track your progress regularly. Adjust your approach as needed, and don't be afraid to pivot if you discover new goals or strategies that better suit you.

30. **Prioritize Continuous Learning**: Wealth-building is a lifelong journey. Stay informed by reading books, taking advanced courses, following market trends, and discussing ideas with financial mentors or a community of like-minded individuals.

Embracing a Wealth Mindset

Sustainable financial success goes beyond strategies and numbers; it's a mindset. A wealth mindset helps you approach challenges positively, continuously seek growth, and view finances as a tool for a fulfilled life.

31. **Resilience and Adaptability**: Markets fluctuate, personal circumstances change, and setbacks happen. A wealth mindset embraces resilience, viewing these challenges as learning experiences.

32. **Generosity and Legacy**: True wealth often extends beyond personal gain. Consider how you can use your financial knowledge and success to positively impact others, whether through philanthropy, mentoring, or creating a financial legacy for future generations.

33. **Personal Fulfillment and Growth**: Financial independence is a powerful tool to enrich your life. With financial security, explore personal goals, hobbies, and interests that bring you joy and fulfillment.

Final Thoughts: Your Path Forward

You've put in the work to understand financial strategies, clarify your goals, and learn how to manage and grow wealth. Your journey toward wealth mastery doesn't end here—it's a continuous process of growth, learning, and evolution. By applying these principles consistently, you're positioning yourself for a lifetime of financial success and security.

Take this newfound knowledge and confidence, and embark on your path to financial independence with purpose and clarity. Your future self will thank you for the choices you make today. Here's to your success on the journey of wealth mastery and financial freedom!

BONUS CONTENT- Further Areas of Study

Below are 15 areas of further study that I highly recommend you look into after reading this book. They will only further strengthen your mind and help you complete your WEALTH MASTERY.

1. Case Studies of Real-World Wealth Journeys

Description: Including case studies adds relatability, illustrating real-life examples of individuals at various financial stages and showing their wealth-building journeys. Each story can reveal unique challenges, strategies, and turning points, offering readers inspiration and practical takeaways for their own paths. Case studies work well across different backgrounds and income levels, highlighting that wealth can be built from various starting points.

Content:
34. **Background**: Start by introducing each person's financial situation and goals. For example, someone might have started with student debt, while another may have begun with limited savings. Include specific demographics (e.g., age, education, income bracket) to create a relatable narrative.

35. **Strategies Used**: Explain the steps each individual took, such as aggressive debt repayment, building multiple income streams, frugal living, or high-risk investing. For someone who was earning a low income, this might mean shifting career paths, adding a side hustle, or investing in further education. Another case might involve someone using passive income strategies to grow wealth while focusing on a fulfilling career.
36. **Lessons Learned**: Highlight key insights each individual gained, such as the importance of patience, avoiding get-rich-quick schemes, or taking calculated risks.
37. **Outcome**: Share their progress toward financial independence, whether they're financially free, semi-retired, or on track to achieve their goals. Case studies can conclude with their advice to readers.

2. Visualization and Goal-Setting Techniques

Description: Visualization and goal-setting are powerful tools for making abstract financial goals feel achievable. By visualizing, readers create a mental image of their ideal financial state, making it easier to stay motivated and aligned with daily financial decisions.

Content:
38. **Visualization Techniques**: Explain techniques such as vision boards, which help readers stay focused on specific financial goals like buying a house, achieving debt freedom, or building an investment portfolio. Vision boards can incorporate pictures, quotes, and affirmations, acting as a daily reminder of what they're working towards. Journaling is another technique where readers write down goals and the feelings associated with achieving them, reinforcing their importance.
39. **SMART Goals**: Introduce SMART (Specific, Measurable, Achievable, Relevant, Time-Bound) goals to transform vague aspirations into tangible objectives. For instance, instead of "save more money," a SMART goal would be "save $5,000 for an emergency fund in six months by saving $834 monthly."
40. **Tracking and Celebrating Progress**: Encourage readers to track their progress and celebrate small milestones, such as saving $1,000 or investing in their first stock. Tracking keeps readers accountable, while celebration reinforces positive habits. Techniques like setting up monthly financial reviews or using goal-tracking apps can provide structure and keep readers engaged with their journey.

3. Money and Relationships

Description: Money plays a pivotal role in relationships, from partnerships to friendships to family dynamics. Money-related stress or conflict can arise if there are no clear boundaries, open communication, or shared goals. This section explores how readers can manage these dynamics to foster healthy financial relationships.

Content:

41. **Financial Transparency with Partners**: Discuss the importance of discussing finances with partners openly, covering topics like shared and separate accounts, budgeting, and debt. Provide tips for setting financial goals together, such as monthly "money dates" where couples review expenses, savings, and investments, ensuring they remain aligned.
42. **Setting Boundaries with Family/Friends**: Offer strategies for managing financial boundaries, like deciding on a budget for gifts or politely declining loans to family and friends. It's especially important for readers to have preset boundaries to avoid financial strain or resentment.
43. **Teaching Financial Literacy to Children**: For readers with children, outline age-appropriate ways to educate kids about money. For younger kids, this could mean introducing simple concepts like saving allowance in a jar, while teenagers can learn about budgeting, bank accounts, and even investing basics. Early financial literacy lessons empower children to build sound money habits and an appreciation for delayed gratification.

4. Financial Tools and Apps

Description: Financial tools and apps can streamline budgeting, goal-tracking, and investing, making it easier for readers to stay organized and make informed decisions. Technology can simplify the financial process, removing some of the intimidation associated with money management.

Content:
44. **Budgeting Apps**: Explain how apps like YNAB (You Need a Budget), Mint, and PocketGuard can help readers track spending, set budgets, and plan for future expenses. Each app has unique features; for example, YNAB focuses on giving every dollar a job, while Mint connects to bank accounts for real-time tracking.
45. **Investment Platforms**: Introduce accessible investment platforms like Robinhood and Vanguard, covering their specific use cases. Robinhood's user-friendly design can appeal to beginner investors, while Vanguard's range of index funds and ETFs might suit readers interested in long-term, diversified investments. Describe how automated services, like Acorns, can round up spare change to invest, making investing simple.
46. **Net Worth Trackers**: Highlight tools like Personal Capital that enable readers to track net worth by connecting various accounts, including checking, savings, and investments. Tracking net worth is a way for readers to measure financial health over time, celebrating progress toward wealth-building goals.

5. The Psychology of Wealth in Different Cultures

Description: Wealth and financial behavior are often shaped by cultural beliefs. Exploring how different cultures approach wealth can help readers examine their beliefs, recognize limiting attitudes, and adopt new perspectives.

Content:
47. **Comparative Overview**: Discuss common wealth-related attitudes across cultures. For instance, Japanese Kakeibo budgeting emphasizes thoughtful spending, while American culture often values individual wealth accumulation and achievement. Some European countries prioritize work-life balance over maximizing income, showing that wealth isn't solely about accumulation but also about lifestyle alignment.
48. **Money Belief Reflection**: Encourage readers to examine their own beliefs and values surrounding wealth. Cultural conditioning can shape beliefs, like associating wealth with selfishness or seeing debt as inherently negative. Recognizing these beliefs can empower readers to reshape limiting attitudes and develop a wealth mindset aligned with their personal values.
49. **Incorporating Positive Beliefs**: Offer examples of beneficial financial practices from different cultures that readers might adopt. Japanese mindfulness techniques, for instance, can help readers develop a thoughtful approach to budgeting, while a European-style focus on work-life balance can promote a lifestyle centered on quality of life over material accumulation.

6. Advanced Investment Strategies

Description: For readers who want to go beyond basic investing, advanced strategies offer opportunities for higher returns and diversification. This section introduces more complex assets and investment types.

Content:
50. **REITs and Commodities**: Real estate investment trusts (REITs) allow investors to buy shares in real estate assets, making property investment more accessible. Explain how REITs work, including their potential for dividends and their role in a balanced portfolio. Commodities, such as gold, silver, or oil, can be a hedge against inflation. Introduce the concept of commodity funds or direct purchases for those interested.
51. **Cryptocurrency Basics**: Offer an overview of cryptocurrency, from popular coins like Bitcoin and Ethereum to the risks of investing in digital currency. Introduce readers to crypto wallets, security measures, and the volatility associated with this asset class, emphasizing the importance of a conservative approach when diversifying with crypto.
52. **Options Trading**: Options are contracts that give investors the right to buy or sell stocks at a predetermined price. Options can be used to generate income, hedge investments, or leverage positions. Due to complexity and risk, emphasize a cautious

approach for readers and recommend educating themselves thoroughly before engaging in options trading.

7. The Impact of Economic Cycles on Wealth-Building

Description: Economic cycles influence job security, investment returns, and consumer confidence, all of which affect personal finance. This section teaches readers how to adjust their strategies according to economic conditions.

Content:
53. **Understanding Recession and Boom Cycles**: Describe how economies fluctuate between periods of growth (booms) and contraction (recessions). Highlight how these cycles impact job markets, interest rates, and stock markets, helping readers understand why adjustments in personal finance may be necessary.
54. **Adjusting Investment Strategies**: Explain strategies for managing investments in different economic climates, such as adopting a more conservative approach during recessions or taking advantage of market downturns to buy undervalued assets. Readers can use market cycles to their advantage by knowing when to invest conservatively and when to take calculated risks.
55. **Emergency Funds for Economic Downturns**: Emphasize the importance of having an emergency fund for unexpected downturns. During a recession, this can act as a buffer, allowing readers to avoid tapping into investments or going into debt. An emergency fund should ideally cover three to six months of living expenses, offering peace of mind and financial stability during uncertain times.

8. Philanthropy and Wealth

Description: This section delves into how wealth can be used for philanthropy, allowing readers to create a legacy that reflects their values. Philanthropy enriches lives not just through giving, but by enhancing a sense of purpose and contribution.

Content:
56. **Types of Giving**: Cover different forms of charitable contributions, including direct donations, setting up charitable trusts, and establishing foundations. Direct donations to causes, crowdfunding campaigns, or community organizations offer a simple way to make an impact, while charitable trusts and foundations provide avenues for more structured giving and may include tax benefits. For instance, a donor-advised fund allows people to make charitable contributions and receive immediate tax deductions.
57. **Tax Benefits**: Explore how donations can reduce taxable income, making philanthropy beneficial both for communities and for financial planning. Explain common deductions and how gifts like appreciated stock or real estate can maximize

tax savings. Readers will benefit from understanding the practical aspects of giving, especially when it's aligned with tax planning.
58. **Choosing Causes**: Suggest how readers can align their giving with their personal values, maximizing impact and satisfaction. Encourage them to reflect on causes close to their hearts, whether it's environmental, social justice, education, or healthcare-related. Highlight the importance of researching charities to ensure that contributions are going to reputable organizations and making a real difference.

9. Health and Wealth Connection

Description: Health and wealth are closely linked, as physical and mental wellness directly impact financial habits, productivity, and decision-making. This section explores the idea that achieving financial success can be easier when one is healthy.

Content:
59. **Physical Health and Financial Habits**: Explain how healthy habits often translate into disciplined financial practices. Readers who prioritize regular exercise, balanced nutrition, and sleep may notice improvements in productivity, focus, and resilience—qualities that also benefit financial planning. Simple lifestyle changes like meal prepping or prioritizing preventive health can yield both physical and financial benefits.
60. **Mental Health and Money Mindset**: Address how stress, anxiety, and depression can lead to impulsive or avoidant financial behaviors, such as emotional spending or ignoring bills. Recommend practical approaches like mindfulness practices, therapy, or journaling to promote mental health and help readers feel more in control of their finances. For instance, meditation or even five minutes of daily mindfulness can help readers become more aware of spending triggers.
61. **Healthy Lifestyle Tips**: Provide budget-friendly lifestyle advice, such as how to save on groceries, meal plan, or engage in low-cost fitness activities. Small changes like incorporating more home-cooked meals or finding free outdoor workouts can help readers maintain a healthy body and bank balance, reinforcing the idea that health is a foundational part of wealth.

10. Dealing with Financial Setbacks

Description: Financial setbacks are a common part of wealth-building. This section focuses on resilience and actionable steps for readers to overcome challenges, rebuild, and maintain a positive outlook.

Content:
62. **Creating a Contingency Plan**: Discuss how to set up a buffer for emergencies, such as saving a percentage of monthly income or maintaining a separate savings account. A strong contingency plan can include knowing which expenses to cut first, having a

cash flow management strategy, and understanding which investments could be liquidated quickly if necessary.
63. **Rebuilding Financially**: Offer guidance on prioritizing debt, generating additional income, and gradually rebuilding savings. For example, readers could start by addressing high-interest debts to improve cash flow, seek side hustles to increase income, or allocate small amounts to an emergency fund. Small steps compound over time, and a gradual approach prevents burnout and keeps goals manageable.
64. **Staying Positive**: Share mindset practices like gratitude journaling, visualization, and reframing to keep a positive outlook during challenging financial times. Encourage readers to see setbacks as learning experiences rather than failures. Reminding themselves of their financial goals, maintaining gratitude for what's going well, and surrounding themselves with a supportive community can help readers persevere through difficulties.

11. Building Wealth Through Intellectual Property

Description: Intellectual property (IP) can be a valuable asset, generating passive income and expanding one's financial portfolio. This section introduces IP types, the process of creating IP, and ways to protect and monetize it.

Content:
65. **Types of Intellectual Property**: Define different types of IP, such as copyrights, patents, and trademarks. Copyrights protect creative works like books, music, or films, while patents protect inventions, and trademarks safeguard brand identity through logos or names. Discuss how readers can identify which IPs might be suitable for their talents or business ventures.
66. **Digital Products**: Walk readers through creating monetizable digital products, like e-books, courses, and software. For instance, a photographer might create a digital portfolio of stock photos for licensing, or a writer might publish an e-book on Amazon Kindle. The initial effort of creating digital content can yield ongoing income without additional effort.
67. **Protecting IP**: Explain the importance of copyrighting or patenting work to prevent unauthorized use. A basic guide on how to copyright an e-book, trademark a logo, or patent an invention helps readers understand how to secure their IP assets, ensuring they maximize the financial benefit of their creativity.

12. Creating an Ethical Wealth Plan

Description: Ethical wealth planning involves making financial choices that positively impact society and reflect personal values. This section covers ways to invest, spend, and save responsibly.

Content:

68. **Ethical Investment Choices**: Introduce Environmental, Social, and Governance (ESG) investing, where readers can support companies committed to sustainability and social responsibility. Describe mutual funds or exchange-traded funds (ETFs) that prioritize ethical investments. This allows readers to align their portfolios with their values, investing in companies that promote green energy or community-focused programs.
69. **Supporting Local and Sustainable Businesses**: Highlight the benefits of shopping locally or choosing brands with transparent and ethical practices. Explain how spending decisions can have a social impact, such as supporting small businesses in their community. Additionally, highlight how choosing sustainable products may be better for the planet and potentially more cost-effective over the long term.
70. **Balancing Wealth and Values**: Offer strategies for ensuring wealth-building aligns with core values, from donating a percentage of earnings to meaningful causes to practicing conscious consumerism. Encourage readers to create a "wealth mission statement" that outlines their goals, values, and how they intend to give back, reminding them that wealth can be a tool for creating positive change.

13. Estate Planning Basics

Description: Estate planning ensures that accumulated wealth benefits loved ones and organizations that reflect personal values. This section provides readers with foundational knowledge on estate planning.

Content:
71. **Wills and Trusts**: Explain the importance of a will and introduce different types of trusts, such as living trusts that can help minimize probate time. A will designates how assets will be distributed, while trusts can offer tax advantages, privacy, and asset protection. Understanding the basics helps readers see estate planning as a proactive, wealth-preserving step.
72. **Passing Down Wealth**: Detail options for passing on wealth to children or other beneficiaries, such as setting up custodial accounts or investing in 529 education plans. Highlight the advantages of early planning and communication to prevent potential conflicts.
73. **Legacy Planning**: Encourage readers to think beyond material wealth by documenting values, family stories, or life lessons to pass down. Legacy planning ensures that wealth and wisdom are transferred, creating a richer family heritage. Suggest ways readers can preserve family values, from creating family mission statements to recording life advice in letters.

14. Negotiating Skills for Financial Success

Description: Effective negotiation skills can improve earning potential, reduce expenses, and foster confidence in various financial dealings. This section covers negotiation tactics in both career and daily scenarios.

Content:
74. **Salary Negotiation**: Offer a step-by-step guide on negotiating raises or benefits during job interviews or performance reviews. Emphasize research, preparation, and presenting value-added contributions as key to success. Discuss setting a target salary, practicing negotiation conversations, and responding to counteroffers.
75. **Everyday Negotiation**: Show how negotiation skills can be useful beyond salary discussions, such as when purchasing a car, negotiating rent, or seeking discounts on services. Encourage readers to research market prices, ask for discounts, and be willing to walk away if terms don't meet their budget.
76. **Confidence-Building**: Teach readers ways to build negotiation confidence, like rehearsing, recognizing their worth, and focusing on the long-term gains of standing firm in negotiations. Emphasize the importance of a positive mindset, preparation, and knowing when to compromise to reach a win-win situation.

15. Leveraging Tax Efficiency

Description: Tax efficiency is a powerful wealth-building tool that allows readers to maximize income and retain more earnings. This section introduces methods for optimizing tax savings, particularly through strategic account use and deductions.

Content:
77. **Tax-Advantaged Accounts**: Explain the benefits of contributing to tax-advantaged accounts like 401(k)s, IRAs, and HSAs, including tax deferrals and deductions. For example, contributions to a traditional IRA can be tax-deductible, reducing taxable income, while growth within the account is tax-free until withdrawn.
78. **Tax Deductions and Credits**: List common deductions and credits, such as those for mortgage interest, education expenses, or charitable contributions. Educate readers on itemizing deductions vs. taking the standard deduction, helping them make informed choices that fit their situation.
79. **Tax-Loss Harvesting**: Introduce tax-loss harvesting as a method to offset gains with losses in an investment portfolio, reducing taxable income. Explain how selling underperforming investments can generate tax savings, freeing capital to reinvest in higher-growth assets. Encourage consulting a tax advisor to make the most of this advanced strategy.

These sections should offer a well-rounded exploration of wealth-building, covering practical tips and in-depth strategies that empower readers to build, protect, and purposefully use their wealth.

www.ingramcontent.com/pod-product-compliance
Lightning Source LLC
Chambersburg PA
CBHW070424240526
45472CB00020B/1186